THE ICONOGRAPHY OF THE BṚHADĪŚVARA TEMPLE

Dr. FRANÇOISE L'HERNAULT

THE ICONOGRAPHY OF THE BṚHADĪŚVARA TEMPLE

Edited by
LALIT M. GUJRAL

INDIRA GANDHI NATIONAL CENTRE FOR THE ARTS
NEW DELHI

ÉCOLE FRANÇAISE D'EXTRÊME-ORIENT
PONDICHERRY

ARYAN BOOKS INTERNATIONAL
NEW DELHI

THE ICONOGRAPHY OF THE BṚHADĪŚVARA TEMPLE

ISBN-81-7305-220-4

First published in **2002** by
INDIRA GANDHI NATIONAL CENTRE FOR THE ARTS
Central Vista Mess, Janpath, New Delhi-110 001 (India)

ÉCOLE FRANÇAISE D'EXTRÊME-ORIENT
Pondicherry
and
ARYAN BOOKS INTERNATIONAL
Pooja Apts., 4B, Ansari Road, Darya Ganj, New Delhi-110 002 (India)
Tel. : 3287589, 3255799; Fax : 91-11-3270385; E-mail : aryanbooks@vsnl.com

Computer Typeset at ABI Prints & Publishing Co., New Delhi
Printed in India at B.B.N. Printers, New Delhi

Preface

Sometime back, the Indira Gandhi National Centre for the Arts (IGNCA) launched two projects under its programme of *Kṣetra Sampadā*. These projects envisaged not only a set of a specific place or a temple and its units, but its impact on culture of the people surrounding it, the process of interlocking of the devotional, artistic, geographical, socio-political and economic aspects of a particular centre. Two areas identified for such integrated studies were Tanjavur in South and Vrindavana in North India. These in-depth and multidimensional studies of identified areas and monuments resulted in the publication of *Tanjavur Bṛhadīśvara: An Architectural Study*, by Pierre Pichard, in 1995; and *Govindadeva: A Dialogue in Stone*, edited by Margaret Case, in 1996.

Concurrently, started as part of the programme on Chola architecture, undertaken some years back by École Française D'Extrême - Orient (EFEO), Pondicherry, the architectural study of the Bṛhadīśvara temple found a wider meaning in the comprehensive project launched by Dr. Kapila Vatsyayan, then Academic Director, at the IGNCA, to investigate the multi-layered and multi-dimensional personality of the Bṛhadīśvara temple. The temple at Tanjavur is unanimously regarded as the greatest masterpiece of Chola architecture. The artistic excellence of the temple lies in the perfect balance of the parts and the whole, the architecture, sculpture, painting, the stone and bronze images, the idols within, and reliefs without. The temple was constructed roughly between A.D. 995 and 1010 by King Rajārāja I, who ruled from A.D. 985 to 1014.

The temple at Gangaikondacholapuram (henceforth designated as Gangai) was built 20 years later by Rajārāja's son King Rājendra I. The latter in his endeavour to extend the limits of his kingdom despatched an army on a daring raid to the north to the banks of the river Gaṅgā. He decided to construct a royal temple at the new capital some 60 kilometres to the north-west of Tanjavur which was named Gangaikondacholapuram, 'the town of the Chola who took the Gaṅgā'. The temple at Gangai is closely related to the Bṛhadīśvara temple by its architectural composition and they both represent a pair in Chola architecture.

Coordinated by Dr. R. Nagaswamy, a standard code was devised so that all subsequent studies under the project would follow it. One of the inter-related modules of the project includes iconographical study of sculpture, stone reliefs, bronze images and mural paintings. Accordingly, Dr. Françoise L'Hernault of EFEO was entrusted with the task of photo documentation of the icons of the Bṛhadīśvara temple. She photographed each icon on each face of the main temple tower and other shrines. She completed the assignment in 1994 and based on nearly 600 photographs of the icons, she prepared a monograph indicating location of these images as a catalogue for the identification of the iconographical forms on the Bṛhadīśvara temple. The monograph prepared by her sheds illuminating light on the iconographical forms of the two capital sites of the Cholas — Tanjavur and Gangai.

Unfortunately, Dr. Françoise L'Hernault passed away in 1999, before her findings, analyses and the beautiful photographs she took, could be published. It was decided to publish her monograph after careful editing; the format, design, etc. are the same as that of its companion volume *Tanjavur Bṛhadīśvara: An Architectural Study.*

We are grateful to Dr. Kapila Vatsyayan, who conceived and directed execution of the whole project; Dr. N.R. Shetty, Member Secretary, extended all encouragement for the publication of this monograph; and Ms. Krishna Dutt, who had coordinated the entire project with EFEO. Lastly, Mr. Vikas Arya, our co-publisher, is to be thanked for bringing out this beautiful illustrated book.

June 28, 2001 **Lalit M. Gujral**

Contents

The Iconography of the Bṛhadīśvara Temple

The character of the iconography at Tanjavur represents an exception in the Chola world at the end of the tenth and beginning of the eleventh century, and does not fail to amaze and leave one perplexed. One asks oneself if there had been a veritable iconographic programme, or if the iconography was adapted to a monument which was extraordinary through both its architectural conception and its dimensions.

One also asks why Tanjavur and Gangaikondacholapuram (henceforth designated as Gangai), two temples in close proximity both in time and space and having comparable dimensions, exhibit beyond their common points well-known iconographic differences. Under the first Cholas, the presence of a divine figure on each of the three façades of the sanctuary-tower was an established principle, and there was one figure on both façades of the vestibule *(ardha maṇḍapa)*. But, shortly before the reign of Rājarāja, three figures appeared on each façade of the vestibule.

In Tanjavur and Gangai, all the divine figures are transferred to the outer walls of the sanctuary-tower, for the entrance hall is very little developed and its lateral façades are occupied by a stairway and a door guarded by immense doorkeepers *(dvārapāla)*, leaving no place for other iconography.

By way of its very abundance, the iconography of Tanjavur and Gangai is certainly uncommon, but to understand it better, it is necessary to consider it in a wider perspective.

1. THE ICONOGRAPHIC CONTEXT OF TANJAVUR AND GANGAI

The outer walls of the sanctuary-tower are known, prior to Rājarāja, to have most generally included Dakṣiṇāmūrti in the south and Brahmā in the north, on the western façade Viṣṇu or Ardhanārīśvara, or, above all from the tenth century onwards, the Liṅgodbhavamūrti. The two façades of the vestibule represent in most cases Gaṇapati and Durgā; but, beginning with Uttama Chola (A.D. 969-985), the iconography of the vestibules becomes more extensive and three niches with divine figures occupy each of the two façades. In one case, at the end of the tenth century, Agastya is present (Figure 1) and one finds in the south Gaṇapati, Naṭarāja and Agastya, while in the north are Bhikṣāṭana, Durgā and Ardhanārīśvara.

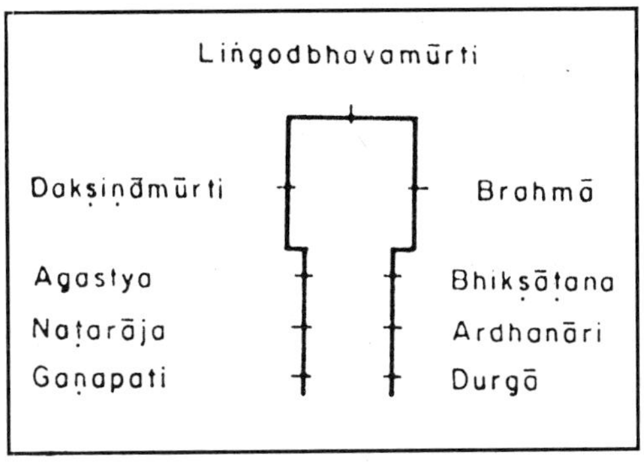

Figure 1. Iconographic plan of the temples at the end of the tenth century (The locations of the deities can follow a different order on each façade: Naṭarāja in the first niche and Gaṇapati in the second, Agastya in the first, etc.)

Agastya is no longer found in temples at the very end of the tenth century and beginning of the eleventh, although, he does appear much later at Melakkadambur and at Darasuram, and the figure which takes his place is Gaṅgādhara. Apart from these temples with three divine figures in the niches

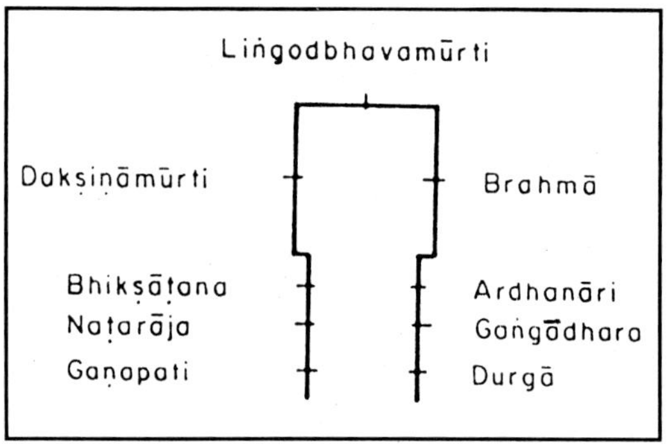

Figure 2. Iconographic plan around the year 1,000 (Same remark concerning order of deities as for Figure 1)

of the sanctuary-tower and with six figures on the walls of the vestibule, a few temples are known which exhibit a large number of deities on the walls of the sanctum: Karandai (Tanjavur taluk), Tiruppurambiyam (Kumbakonam taluk) and Kāmarasa Vaḷḷi (Uḍaiyārpalaiyam taluk.). These three temples dating approximately from the mid-tenth century were modified in order to accommodate a greater number of iconographic representations. Additional niches were made in the walls of the sanctum and the vestibule in the late tenth century and early eleventh century, to judge from their iconographic programmes.

The first observation is that the three temples have introduced a new figure: Kālāri, facing north as in principle befits deities of terrible aspect. One also notes the presence of Subrahmaṇya at Karandai, just as at Cholapuram and at the two Kailāsa in Gangai (these latter three temples are probably contemporaneous and from the period of Rājendra). One thus has the tableau of a series of deities common to the temples of the delta extending into the second half of the tenth century to the era of Rājarāja and Rājendra (Figure 2).

Table - 1 (on page 3) gives the iconography prior to, or nearly contemporaneous with, Tanjavur and Gangai, and in comparison, that of the two latter temples, whereby the walls of the sanctuary-tower and vestibule are not distinguished.

It emerges from Table - 1 that the most common deities of the period around Tanjavur and Gangai are found in those two sanctuaries, with the exception of Agastya.

A great innovation is the presence of numerous subshrines, thirty-six at Tanjavur and thirty-two at Gangai, in the enclosure gallery of the temple. In Tanjavur, they accommodate, other than the eight Lords of the directions, deities of the divine court of Śiva, most of which have now vanished.

2. THE SANCTUARY-TOWER

The Liṅga in the Sanctum

The centre of the sanctum is occupied by an imposing liṅga which is 3.95 metres in height and 1.90 metres in diameter and inserted in a round socle, the spout of which nearly touches the inner northern wall of the sanctum. Originally called Rājarājeśvaram (the Lord of Rājarāja), in the course of the seventeenth century, the name Periya Uḍaiyār Nāyanār (the Great Lord), or Peruvuḍaiyār, was taken, of which Bṛhadīśvara is the Sanskrit equivalent. The liṅga at Gangai, which is just as large, also bears at present the name Bṛhadīśvara. One encounters in several temples in Tamilnadu another type of liṅga, the name of which is derived from its size, Bhīmeśvara, for Bhīma is reputed for his large size and extraordinary physical exploits.

It would appear that for the same reason the liṅga of the Draksharama (tenth century) is called Bhīmeśvara. There, the very large liṅga in the sanctum on the ground floor emerges in the sanctum on the upper storey where the worship is performed. In Tanjavur, the principle of the upper storey sanctum is taken up again, but devoid of its meaning as this sanctum

TABLE - 1

		Tanjavur ground-floor	*Tanjavur upper storey*	*Gangai ground-floor*	*Gangai upper storey*
Common figures around the period of Tanjavur and Gangai	Dakṣiṇāmūrti			*	*
	Brahmā			*	*
	Liṅgodbhava	* *		*	*
	Viṣṇu	*		*	
	Durgā	*		*	
	Gaṇapati	*		*	
	Agastya				
	Naṭarāja	* *		*	
	Bhikṣāṭana	*		*	*
	Ardhanāri	*		*	
	Gaṅgādhara	*		*	*
	Kālāri	*		*	*
Less common figures	Āliṅgana	*			
	Vṛṣavāhana				
	Subrahmaṇya			*	
	Bhairava			**	
	Vīṇādhara				
Figures specific to Tanjavur and Gangai	Harihara	*		*	
	Sūrya	*			*
	Candra	*			*
	Lakṣmī	*		*	
	Sarasvatī	*		*	
	Aghora	**			
	Candraśekhara	**			
	Vīrabhadra	*			
	Śiva	*			
	Tripurāntaka	*	*		
	Viṣṇuanugraha			*	
	Kāmāntaka			*	
	Caṇḍeśanugraha			*	
	Dikpāla				*
	11 Rudra				*
	Bhūvarāha				*
	Gajāntaka				*
	Devī-Vamādeva	*			

contains nothing. The liṅga is in the only sanctum on the ground floor, but because of its large size, a system of scaffoldage allows the priests access to the summit of the liṅga to perform ablutions.

The Iconography of the Corridor on the Ground Floor of the Sanctuary-tower

Like the two superposed sanctums, resembling those of the Draksharama temple, the ambulatory with four cardinal openings appears to also come from Andhra, from the Bhīmeśvara in Chebrolu (tenth century). The principle was, however, previously not unknown, as borne witness by the Vaikuṇṭha Perumāḷ in Kanchipuram, the Sundareśvara in Uttiramerur, the Kailāsanātha in Tiruppattur and the Narttamalai temple.

However, it does not appear to have been firmly established in Tamilnadu, for it is sometimes blind, as in the Kailāsanātha in Kanchipuram and at Gangai, which is the last existing example of a temple with a surrounding corridor.

Despite the feeble lighting given by the axial openings, the inner and outer walls of the corridor in Tanjavur are covered with paintings, interrupted by large stone figures of deities on the level of the openings. Such figures belong both to the ambulatory and, because they can be seen from there, to the façades of the sanctuary-tower. Apart from the liṅga visible from the eastern entrance, of which we have spoken, there are three other large sculptures.

The conception according to which the supreme god emanates everywhere in the world is architecturally expressed by a sanctuary from which the deities are viewed from the four sides, or by the philosophico-religious notion of Śiva who manifests himself as Sadāśiva and Maheśa in the liṅga. Śiva is composed of five entities invoked during worship, the *pañca brahmā*: Tat Puruṣa, Aghora, Sadyojāta, Vāmadeva and Īśāna. In fact, Sadāśiva is only a mental representation, or rather a mental construction, created by worship. The god is "made of *mantras,* or formulae", that is to say, powers which the formulae have brought forth (Īsana, Tat-Purûṣa, etc.).[1] In Sadāśiva, one distinguishes parts (heads, faces, arms, etc.) which are aspects of the power of the god.

The iconographic translation takes the form of the large figures of Śiva, either with three or four heads, at Elephanta, Ellora or Aurangabad, as well as the liṅga with four or five faces. In Tanjavur, the iconographic rendering is different, as there is a deity in each cardinal niche, with the exception in the east where the door of the sanctum is located. As for the fifth head, Iśāna at the top facing the heavens, it is possible that the empty upper storey sanctum was conceived as his abode.

According to a temple inscription, a bronze ordered by Rājarāja bore the name *Pañcadeha* (Śiva with five bodies).[2] One of the five bodies, larger than the others, had ten arms, and the four other smaller bodies each had four arms. This *Pañcadeha*, of which no concrete representation is known, is unmistakably a visual variation of the concept of Sadāśiva.

There are representations of this concept in yet different forms on numerous gateways to temples from the seventeenth, eighteenth and nineteenth centuries. While the towers of these gateways bear deities made of brick and lime mortar, two deities are found on each side of the doorway on the lower level: one is known as Sadāśiva, a seated Śiva with five heads and ten hands bearing weapons; the other is a goddess, also with five heads and ten arms, called Manonmanī.

Rudra-Aghora (southern façade) (Plates 2, 3, 4)

This is a seated Śiva with two arms (310 cm in height) holding trident and sword, locally called Jvaradeva, a name which is not very old, but indicates that the god was conceived of as terrible (Jvaradeva: *jvara:* "fever"), like the Aghora Śiva of the *pañca brahmā*, which is confirmed by the warlike attributes, the sword and the trident. The niche is flanked by two small male attendants on the pilasters.

Dancing Śiva-Sadyojāta (western façade)

Śiva is within an aureola of flames, similar to the aureola of processional bronzes. He has two feet on the ground and his legs are bent to form a square (the *catura tāṇḍava* posture). The hands of his ten arms hold mainly warlike attributes. These are, from top to bottom:

Right hands		*Left hands*
mace	-	small trident
thunderbolt (recent stucco)	-	noose
sword	-	shield
gesture of fearlessness	-	arm thrown across the chest

Pārvatī is standing to his left on the pilaster bordering the niche. On the pilaster opposite the niche, divided in three rows, are squatting gaṇas and a four-armed Tāṇḍu beating the drum. This dance has the semblance of a fearsome dance. Is it a dance corresponding to a myth in which the god is involved? Because of the importance of Tripurāntaka in the temple, and despite the absence of Skanda in the arms of Pārvatī, one could think, among other interpretations, that it depicts the dance called *Tripuratāṇḍava.*

Goddess Vāmadeva (northern façade)

The goddess, seated in the lotus posture, with rosary and lotus in her hands, is locally likened to Gāyatrī. She represents the feminine aspect of Śiva in the *pañca brahmā* system. She is located in the north, thus to the left of the liṅga in the sanctum, the place customarily reserved for the consort. Rosary and lotus are the two attributes generally held by the goddess in her shrines in the Śiva temples of the region. The niche is flanked by two small female attendants on the pilasters, a proof that the central deity is Vāmadeva but also the goddess.

Visual Representation of two Interlocking Concepts

If the fearsome aspect of Aghora and the feminine (Vāmadeva) aspect are easily identifiable on the large statues of Śiva at Elephanta, Ellora and Aurangabad, this is not the case for Sadyojāta, and the presence of a dancing Śiva on the western façade in Tanjavur is rather puzzling. This is not, however, an innovation in the South Indian world, as one finds among the Pallava three representations of Śiva in the sanctuary: Śiva Dakṣiṇāmūrti in the south, Śiva Yogīśvara in the north and dancing Śiva on the back façade. This was probably due to the influence of the *Tirumantram* of Tirumūlar, around the sixth century, according to which the parāmananda *tāṇḍava*, the process of cosmic creation, embodies the fivefold activities of the god, the *pañcakṛtya* (creation, preservation, destruction, veiling, release or grace). The question is to know why dancing Śiva is on the western façade. Perhaps because it was known that Aghora and Vāmadeva had clearly designated locations? But, in any case, one is in the presence of two very intimately connected concepts, embedded in a rare iconic structure: Sadāśiva, who combines the five entities comprising the *pañca brahmā*, and Śiva, whose dance is the essence of the five-fold activities of the universe.

Before and after Tanjavur, it was customary to put Śiva born of the liṅga-pillar of fire (Liṅgodbhavamūrti) on the back façade (generally west). If one accepts that theological conceptions can receive approximate iconographic translations, one understands quite clearly that the supreme Śiva, the Śiva of the *ānanda tāṇḍava* who dances eternally in the ether *(ākāśa),* could have been in the place of the Liṅgodbhavamūrti, the infinite pillar. Accordingly, the upper storey sanctum with its 108 dance postures could only be conceived as ether, *ākāśa,* the space of Śiva's dance.

In fact, from the iconographic point of view, the interpenetration of concepts appears twice: Sadyojāta, but also supreme Śiva, Lord of dance, and Īśāna in the ether, but also ether as the place of the cosmic dance.

It is difficult to explain the presence of two dancing Śivas: one in the west and the other in the south-western corner, with four arms, on the outer façade. One might suppose that the one in the south-western corner was a well-established form on the southern façades of sanctuaries before Tanjavur, and that it was held to be necessary from an iconographic point of view, whereas the dancing Śiva in the west is veritably a conception of theologians, absolutely unique.

The Paintings (done by another party)

The Iconography of the Façades on the Ground Floor of the Sanctuary-tower

The figures will be presented in the direction of circumambulation, beginning thus on the right side at the exit of the sanctum, (Plates 2, 3, 4).

Śiva (east)

This is a standing figure which, like Candraśekhara, holds axe and antelope in his upper hands, although the lower hands do not form the postures of boon-conferring or fearlessness, but rather hold rosary and fruit. The right portion of the niche represents three worshippers, but the left side does not contain symmetric sculptures because of the wall of the vestibule which was erected perpendicular to the sanctuary afterwards.

Sūrya (east)

He is standing, aureola around his head. The lotuses he had held in his two hands are broken. Śiva sanctuaries usually do not contain Sūrya, whose subshrine is in temple courtyards. Nevertheless, there is the example of Sūrya on the Dharmarāja *ratha* in Mahabalipuram.

Liṅgapurāṇa deva? or Cakradānamūrti? (east)

The name Liṅgapurāna deva which appears in an inscription could be synonymous with Lingodbhavamūrti, who himself often bears, in several temples, the name Aṇṇāmalaiyār. In the Liṅgodbhavamūrti, Śiva emerges from the liṅga but his feet remain unseen, concealed in the pillar of fire. Here, this is not the case.

In addition, Viṣṇu and Brahmā are present in the Liṅgodbhavamūrti in the forms of boar and swan and/or in human form. Here, only Viṣṇu, hands joined, is kneeling at the feet of Śiva. In fact, the entire sculpture calls to mind the giving of the discus to Viṣṇu by Śiva (Cakradānamūrti). This scene is represented in Gangai where, as is befitting, Śiva and Pārvatī are seated on Kailāsa.

The border of the niche includes no elements which would enable better identification. On one side are two gaṇa musicians, surmounted by a gandharva in flight; and on the other, two women on their knees in the act of salutation are also surmounted by a flying gandharva.

Bhikṣāṭana (south)

The god is naked, hair dishevelled, with four arms and his customary attributes: in the upper hands are kettledrum and a bunch of peacock feathers; one lower hand holds a skull while the fourth touches an antelope standing on its hind legs. Behind the god, a gnome carries a begging bowl; on one side of the niche is the wife of a *ṛṣi*, and on the other are three gnomes from Śiva's retinue.

Vīrabhadra? (south)

The identification of this eight-armed Śiva is problematical. It differs in several points from the eight-armed Bhairava-Kṣetrapāla which is known from about the same period (the Bhairava beneath the Nayak porch, the Bhairava in Tiruvalanjuli, Manambadi, Cholapuram, and in the gopura at Chidambaram). The latter, accompanied by a hound, are naked, covered with serpents and have dishevelled hair, while the god in question has no hound, is clothed, wears his hair in a coil and has a moustache. As regards the attributes of Bhairava-Kṣetrapāla just mentioned, they have six in common: the bow and arrow, sword, shield, trident and skull. The last two attributes can vary: bell, noose, kettledrum, bunch of peacock feathers.

The Śiva Vīrabhadra? of Tanjavur has, from top to bottom, on the right: skull, shield, noose, axe; and on the left: trident, sword, then two unseen attributes, one of which must be an antelope, corresponding symmetrically to the axe. The bow and arrow of the Bhairava with eight arms are thus absent. That this Śiva would be clothed, would be without bow and arrow and would, moreover, be in the midst of other figures in the sanctuary, precludes consideration of it as a Bhairava-Kṣetrapāla. One observes, in effect, that on the four gateways at Chidambaram, Bhairava-Kṣetrapāla is always located in a corner, the corner being seen as a weak point needing protection. The carrying of the skull, although particularly associated with Bhairava, poses no problem, for it is also the attribute of numerous fearsome deities.

There are, nevertheless, few more positive elements for an identification with Vīrabhadra. Apart from Vīrabhadra chief of the Seven Mothers, Vīrabhadra, the destroyer of Dakṣa is represented, well after the Chola period, standing, with four arms and holding the attributes bow and arrow, sword and shield, while at his side is Dakṣa with a ram's head. Preceding these to a certain extent standardized representations, two depictions exist of Vīrabhadra in action, in the act of striking Dakṣa: the representation at the Kailāsa in Kanchipuram and that on the northern stairway in Tanjavur itself. Also known, somewhat less than a century after Tanjavur, is the Vīrabhadra on the outer gateway at Darasuram. It is clearly identified by an inscription, as is Dakṣaprajapati in an adjacent niche. Seated, he holds in his two upper hands a trident and bunch of peacock feathers; the lower hands are broken.

This type of representation is unique and one observes that the gateways at Tiruvanaikka and at Chidambaram, near in time to Darasuram, have no Vīrabhadra.

Kālāntaka (south)

Śiva is in the act of trampling underfoot the god Kāla (Time), pointing a menacing index finger at him, his trident ready to strike. The two upper hands hold a hatchet. At Gangai, Śiva slashes the demon with his hatchet rather than with his trident. There is even a difference between the Ardhanāri in Tanjavur and that in Gangai: in Tanjavur preference is given to the trident, while in Gangai, the axe is chosen.

To the left of the niche, Yama/Kāla is sculpted in pursuit of Mārkaṇḍeya who, on the other side of the niche, embraces the liṅga, his refuge. The two figures, separated by the niche, recall this episode, whereas the representation at Gangai is more realistic. In effect, on a single relief beside the niche, Mārkaṇḍeya embraces the liṅga to escape Yama who drags him along with his lasso.

In Tanjavur, Kālāri is facing south, probably because that is Yama's abode. But in Gangai, he is in the north, the direction in which figures of terrible aspect are located.

There is also a representation of Kālāntaka on a small relief on the inner gateway.

Naṭarāja (south)

Same location in Tanjavur and Gangai. The narrative context of the dance of Śiva is much more elaborate in Gangai than in Tanjavur, and several episodes connected with Naṭarāja are depicted.

The dance of Śiva (*tāṇḍava*), at the origin, is a dance of destruction in which the god unleashes himself, accompanied by hordes of skeletal figures and demonic gnomes. Related to this terrible aspect is the legend of Tiruvalangadu (northern Tamilnadu), in which Śiva and Pārvatī, in the form of Kālī, rival each other in an unbridled dance *(urdhva tāṇḍava),* from which Śiva emerges victorious. But the dance which was in favour throughout the Chola period was the *ānanda tāṇḍava,* the terrible dance of bliss, such as appears in Tanjavur and Gangai. In Gangai, on the same stele, Kālī is depicted in the background of dancing Śiva, representing the competition at Tiruvalangadu; to the left, Bhṛṅgin, a fleshless figure to whom Śiva gave a third leg for support when Pārvatī, jealous of his devotion reserved exclusively for Śiva, deprived him of the flesh of his body.

The iconography thus particularized one of the skeletal figures, as was the case for Kāraikkāl Ammaiyār, a female devotee of Śiva, emaciated as a result of her asceticism. Beneath the niche enshrining Naṭarāja, on a supporting stone of the stele, in the company of three gnome musicians, she sings the glory of Śiva while playing the cymbals.

The combination of the two skeletal figures, Bhṛṅgin and Kāraikkāl Ammaiyār, and the representation of Kālī, are very uncommon; other than in Gangai, it is found at Karandai near Tanjavur, dating from the end of the tenth century, and at Tiruvattaturai, located some forty kilometres from Gangai and dating from the second half of the eleventh century, under Virarājendra, one of the sons of Rājendra.

Around the niche are Pārvatī leaning against Nandin, known by the name Śivakāmāsundarī when she accompanies Naṭarāja dancing the *ānanda tāṇḍava*, Nandikeśvara playing the drum, the sons of Śiva, Gaṇapati on his rat alongside Subrahmaṇya on his peacock and, above, the sun and moon.

In Tanjavur, Naṭarāja is alone in the corner and, to the side, sculpted in the wall, Kāraikkāl Ammaiyār is represented surmounted by a gandharva musician. On the other side is found a drummer, above which is another gandharva.

Harihara (west)

The iconography, if not the location, is the same in Tanjavur and Gangai for the composite figure which bears the hatchet emblematic of Śiva and the conch of Viṣṇu. The difference in garments, short for one, long for the other, is pronounced, but only Tanjavur distinguishes the half-coil for Śiva and the half-tiara for Viṣṇu.

Liṅgodbhavamūrti (west)

This representation of Śiva emerging from the pillar of fire is in the same location as in Gangai. While it is in the south at the Kailāsanātha in Kanchipurarn, it subsequently became customary for it to be in the centre of the western façade, or slightly off-centre as here and in Gangai or Tiruppajanam, when another representation is chosen for the axial niche. It is possible that the west would have been selected for the Liṅgodbhavamūrti because in the *pañca brahmā* system the west is the location of Sadyojāta, born all at once, a name related to the usual characteristic of the liṅga, svayambhū, born spontaneously. In Tanjavur, the Liṅgodbhavamūrti is represented with Viṣṇu-boar digging at the bottom of the pillar of fire, and Brahmā on his swan at the summit. They are also human in form, hands joined as worshippers, located on either side of the niche.

Candraśekhara (west)

This is a standing Śiva with four arms. The back hands are holding axe and antelope, while of the front hands, one assumes the posture of fearlessness *(abhaya)* and the other forms the bestowing pose *(āhūya varada)*. On either side of the niche sages are seated and facing Śiva while the gandharva fly towards him.

Candraśekhara (west)

A second Candraśekhara stands in the next niche. Inscribed in an aureola similar to that of deities in bronze, it differs slightly from the preceding in garments and jewellery.

Ardhanārīśvara (north)

This androgynous form of Śiva is almost always accompanied by a bull, hypostasis of Śiva and symbol of his creative power. In Tanjavur, the Śiva side of the figure holds the trident; in Gangai, the hatchet. In both temples, the female half, Pārvatī, wears a long garment and holds a lotus in the hand.

Gaṅgādhara (north)

Śiva customarily receives the Gaṅgā in his hair while consoling Pārvatī, who turns away jealous of the river. Gaṅgādhara generally appears in the north, as in this case. But at Gangai, the representation is in the west, in the same location as in the Kailāsanātha in Kanchipuram, while on the upper storey it is in the north even in Gangai. In Tanjavur, Śiva is without Pārvatī at his side, as was the case under the Chalukya and the Pallava. The context of the scene is given by one of the figures of the retinue in the niche, Bhagīrata, who stands on one leg, arms raised, doing penance as the Gaṅgā descends to earth. On the other side is the hound which calls to mind infernal regions.

Śiva (north)

Śiva is standing and holds hatchet and antelope in his upper hands, sword and shield in his lower hands. Even though the latter two attributes would later regularly be in the hands of Vīrabhadra, must one consider this to be Vīrabhadra and call in question the identification of the Vīrabhadra on the southern façade.

Aliṅgana (north)

Śiva, standing, with hatchet and antelope, is clasping Pārvatī around the waist with one hand and appears to hold a flower, the stem of which is clearly visible, in the palm of his fourth hand.

Candra (east)

Like Sūrya, his counterpart, Candra is standing and has a large aureola around his head. One of the two lotuses held in his broken hands is still discernable.

Tripurāntaka (east)

This standing Śiva with four arms carries bow and arrow and, in his upper hands, axe and antelope. This is strange because the thirty-two Tripurāntaka on the upper storey (sanctuary-tower, vestibule and hall) exhibit the trident and a second arrow in the upper hands, and not, as here, axe and antelope.

The doorkeepers *(dvārapāla)*

The doors to the sanctuary and the three axial openings are protected by four-armed doorkeepers which are much larger than the figures of the deities in the niches. Whereas the doorkeepers are generally armed with clubs, the four pairs of doorkeepers in the sanctuary-tower bear different weapons. While the two doorkeepers in the east are leaning on their clubs, the pair in the south are holding thunderbolts. As for the pair in the west, one doorkeeper holds a trident and the other is leaning on a club. The pair in the north are armed with swords.

The recesses on the façades of the ground floor and of the upper floor are occupied by pilasters ensuing of a vase *(kumbha)* and crowned at the top by a small cage *(panjara)* surrounded by gandharvas. This new decorative element, deriving from the ancient and well-known vase of plenty *(pūrṇa kalaśa),* introduced for the first time at Tanjavur was adopted by many temples down to the Nayak and Maratha periods (Plate 18).

The arcatures above the niches consist mostly of a rich, finely chiselled foliage-motive. The semicircular centre is occupied by a figure. Out of some twenty arcatures, seven are unfinished or mutilated, the others have a rather common iconography (Bhikṣāṭana, two Naṭarāja, Caṇḍeśanugrahamūrti, sitting Gaṇapati, dancing Gaṇapati, four seated Śiva, dancing gaṇa, animal worshipping the liṅga, dancer, etc.) (Plate 18).

Out of the some forty blind dormer-windows crowning the cornice of the ground floor, the west is as usual devoted to vaisnava figures: Bhūvarāha, Bakāsuravadha, Narasiṃhavadha. The other saivite figures are of common iconography: Kāmāntaka, Caṇḍeśānugrahamūrti, Naṭarāja, Bhikṣāṭana, Tripurāntaka, Subrahmaṇya, Mahiṣāsuramardinī, Gaṅgādhara, Śiva and Pārvatī seated together, Kaṇṇappa, dancers, sages (Plate 18).

Iconographic Principles or Iconographic Fillers?

The character of grandeur and majesty which the sovereigns wanted to give to their temples is translated by the considerable height of the sanctuary-tower. This height conditioned, and was conditioned by, the plan of the ground floor and of the upper storey, divided by pilasters into spans. The spans, surmounted on the first tier either by aediculae, or by connecting galleries between the aediculae, are alternately projected or recessed; the projections, corresponding to the aediculae, number five on each façade. In Gangai, they are all hewn with niches enshrining a deity, but in Tanjavur the central projection is an opening onto the representation of a deity in a niche on the wall of the sanctum. In both cases, there are thus five deities on each façade. Finally, the number of niches in each façade in Tanjavur and in Gangai appears to be clearly determined by the architectural scale of the monuments, but the number of niches would correspond to the symbolism of the number five for Śiva.

Which figures were retained in Tanjavur and Gangai from the catalogue of earlier temples, and which new figures did they adopt to fill what was unprecedented in earlier architecture: the upper storey of the sanctuary before the tower begins?

The entire layout of earlier temples was drastically changed by reason of the particular architecture of the principal sanctuary-tower in Tanjavur. It is composed on the west-east axial alignment of the sanctuary-tower, of a vestibule with two lateral stairways, of a long pillared hall and a porch from the Nayak period. Because of their architectural vastness, Tanjavur and Gangai required innovations. But, did one follow certain established principles, or did one improvise by drawing from a reserve of potential iconographic forms?

The fact that the earlier façade of the sanctuary-tower had two more figures than in Gangai, and that the figures present in both sanctuaries had different locations, permit one to say that nothing was truly fixed. Thus, Bhikṣāṭana is found in the south in Tanjavur and in the east in Gangai; Ardhanārīśvara is in the north in Tanjavur and in the west in Gangai; Kālārimurti is in the south in Tanjavur and in the north in Gangai; Gaṅgādhara is in the north in Tanjavur and in the west in Gangai; and, Harihara is in the west in Tanjavur and in the south in Gangai.

Finally, Tanjavur has several representations of Śiva which do not belong to the customary iconography. On the eastern façade is a two-armed Śiva with trident, one hand on his hip, and a second Śiva with trident, antelope, rosary and bowl (or fruit?), on the southern façade is a fearsome Śiva with eight arms, a type of Vīrabhadra or Aghora Śiva, but not corresponding to any known form. Finally, on the northern façade is a Śiva which only partially conforms to representations of Vīrabhadra.

The figures in Gangai, on the other hand, are all easily identifiable and of known iconography. But, the installation of the statues occurred at two different times: some when the walls were erected, others later. Is this because there had been a delay in the execution of the statuary, or because the statues installed after the construction of the walls had been ordered by dignitaries who would have proposed their choice of deity? One thinks in particular of the statues of Subrahmaṇya, Bhairava and Kāmāntaka. Because of this, and what was previously said regarding the differences between Tanjavur and Gangai, one can discover no ruling principle for either the choice or the location of the deities.

The Iconography of the Corridor on The Upper Storey of the Sanctuary-tower

The base of the outer wall of the sanctum on the upper storey consists mainly of a high plinth, a succession of stone blocks of 75 cm height, and of a quarter-round finial. The stone blocks bear only rough-hewn sculptures and some blocks remain merely squared and without sculpture (Plate 1).

The sculptures depict dance postures *(karaṇa)* in the form of a four-armed figure, Śiva, who in several cases holds certain of his attributes: trident, hatchet, antelope; sometimes he is accompanied by his gnome musicians who are playing cymbals and blowing conches. On other monuments, the *karaṇa* are presented either by Tāṇḍu (gateway at the Śāraṅgapāṇi temple in Kumbakonam), or by dancers (gateways at Chidambaram, Vriddhachalam, Tiruvannamalai). The tower of the sanctum contains eighty-one representations, but according to the number of unsculpted blocks, one can determine that there would have been 108, which corresponds to the dance units of the *Nāṭyaśāstra* which T.N. Ramachandra attempted to have identified.

The Iconography of the Façades on the Upper Storey of the Sanctuary-tower

The façades of the upper storey of the sanctuary-tower, vestibule and pillared hall contain together thirty-two Śiva-Tripurāntakas (Plates 5, 6). All of them are four-armed, holding bow and arrow in the lower hands, trident and a second arrow in the upper hands. They therefore differ from the Tripurāntakas on the ground floor in the attributes of the upper hands, but also in attire: the thirty-two Tripurāntakas have serpents knotted as belts around chest and hips, whereas the Tripurāntaka on the ground floor is without.

They are standing, two feet on the socle, or one foot on the socle and the other slightly raised and resting on a small lotiform or lion-shaped socle placed on the first socle. A design becomes apparent in the arrangement of the thirty-two Tripurāntakas: those in the four corners of the sanctuary-tower, as well as those in the vestibule and hall, are represented with one foot raised on a small socle, while all the others stand on straight legs (Plate 5).

The prominence of the Tripurāntaka theme is absolutely unique, first because neither the Āgamas nor the Śilpa texts have provision for the repeated installation of one and the same deity. Moreover, other than these numerous sculptures, three narrative scenes relate the combat of Śiva against the Tripura demons: the painting in the northern corridor of the sanctuary-tower, and two stone panels, one on the inner gateway and the other on the side wall of the southern flight of steps leading to the vestibule of the main shrine.[3]

The same emphasis on this theme is seen among the Pallava, for, according to three inscriptions on the Kailāsanātha in Kanchipuram, King Rājasiṃha compares himself to Śiva, vanquisher of the Pura demons.[4] Several temples dating from Rājasiṃha have Tripurāntaka representations. The first is found at Mahabalipuram on the northern façades of the two shrines of the Shore temple. There, the god with the bow in the crook of one elbow is standing in his chariot drawn by two rearing horses. At the same site, a cuboid stone, approximately one metre in height, which was perhaps the base of a flag-staff, shows on each of the four faces a stately Śiva seated on a throne. One Śiva, instead of hatchet and lotus, carries bow and arrow like Tripurāntaka.

In Kanchipuram, a temple from the period of Rājasiṃha has no representations of Tripurāntaka, but bears the name Amareśvara or Tripurāntakeśvara. The nearby Airāvateśvara temple has on the northern façade a Tripurāntaka, with bow in hand, standing on his chariot driven by his charioteer Brahmā. The Kailāsanātha temple contains five Tripurāntakas: three of them, facing north, are eight-armed, standing on the chariot represented laterally, with Brahmā as the charioteer (enclosure wall and façade of the main shrine). Two others, six-armed, facing west, are also standing on a chariot, but this time represented frontally, with two reared horses (on the back wall of one of the eight small shrines arranged in a row at the entrance of the temple complex, and in one of the seven subshrines attached to the main shrine).

The repetition of thirty-two Tripurāntakas on the upper storey of the Bṛhadīśvara raises questions. Does the number thirty-two have a symbolic function? It is known that the architectural diagram of the site, vāstumaṇḍala, accommodates thirty-two deities on its outer border. But, it is also known that the deities which according to ritual are placed around Śiva are not the deities found in the courtyards of the temples. In other words, the maṇḍala is not conceived in the image of the temples or of the universe. In addition, the arrangement of the thirty-two Tripurāntakas does not form an encompassing whole. For this to have been the case, it would have been necessary that the eastern front portion of the pillared hall, destroyed or never built, would have also had Tripurāntakas, like in the back part of the hall in the west. In this case there would have been not thirty-two, but thirty-eight Tripurāntakas. But, if the initial programme had indeed been to install thirty-two Tripurāntakas, this is perhaps by way of simple reference to the symbolic number thirty-two, independently of any specific implication.

Actually, it is rather in the name Tripurāntaka itself that one must seek the reason for the preferential choice of this form of Śiva. Tripura refers to the ancient Vedic tripartition of the world into heaven, earth and intermediary space. In the myth, the demons expel the gods from the cosmos and entrench themselves as in a citadel of three storeys. Only Śiva, setting the world aflame by means of the fire emanating from his third eye, is able to dislodge them. Following the passage of Śiva's purificatory fire, the triple cosmic city is restored to its original splendour. Thus one sees how Tripurāntaka can be assimilated, not only to the king who conquers, but also to the king who upholds the order of the kingdom.

The royal character of Tripurāntaka is even more clearly seen at the Darasuram temple dating from the twelfth century. There, the northern side of the pillared hall has a series of niches, one of which contains Tripurāntaka (now in the Tanjavur museum) and the adjacent niche still contains a female deity exhibiting the attributes of power, the elephant god and the noose. In Karnataka, this goddess is known by the name Bhuvaneśvarī (mistress of the world); in Tamilnadu she is Tripurasundarī or Rajarājesvarī.[5] The two synonymous names clearly indicate a relation to kingship.

However, it is certainly the ritual context which best offers explanation of what Tripurāntaka would represent. Numerous processional bronzes of Tripurāntaka from the eleventh and twelfth centuries are found in temples, mainly those in the Kaveri valley near Tanjavur. At present, none of these bronzes are used for processions and no priest knows on which occasion they were taken out in the past. The fact that these bronzes have fallen into desuetude could be a response to the question they pose. We think that, being assimilated to the king, Tripurāntaka was taken from the temple on the appearance of the king's natal star which according to inscriptions was celebrated in the temples.[6] Independently of that, Somāskanda is the deity at present taken out during the *brahmotsava* of the temples. In daily processions he rides a small chariot or palanquin, and on the seventh or ninth day he rides the monumental wooden chariot. The latter is a particularly majestic procession of the divine family, Śiva, Pārvatī and the infant Skanda, and has points in common with the parading of the royal couple and the young prince. Nevertheless, it is commonly said that the sortie on the large chariot is the combat of Śiva against the Tripura demons (tripurasaṃhāra). This amalgam clearly shows the convergence of the divine and the royal figures.

The Iconography of the Superstructure of the Tower

All the figures of brick and lime mortar which cover the aediculae of the tower are subsequent to the Chola period. The only originally stone statues are, on the four sides, two Nandins on the first tier and two gnomes on the second tier.

The four cardinal niches at the summit of the tower all contain an identical seated Śiva, now covered with lime mortar. In his upper hands are, a constant, the axe in one and fire in the other (figure in the south), on two figures the trident is seen, and the antelope. Between the niches, on the platform supporting the finial, Nandins, in pairs, are facing each other from the corners.

Gangai adopted a more current option in the niches of the summit: Subrahmaṇya in the east, Dakṣiṇāmūrti, Viṣṇu and Brahmā for the other directions.

3. THE TWO LATERAL STAIRWAYS LEADING TO THE VESTIBULE

Two lateral stairways, each with two flights of steps, lead to a landing preceding the doorways of the vestibule.

Between the sanctuary-tower and the pillared hall, the vestibule contains only four plain square monolithic pillars supporting rectangular brackets decorated with low relief dance scenes.

The doorways opening onto the vestibule are guarded by huge *dvārapāla*. They are all in the same posture, one foot placed on the ground, the other resting on a lion, and they all exhibit a single attribute in one of their four hands: the *dvārapāla* at the southern door have a thunderbolt, those at the door in the north have trident and axe.

The string walls confining the two flights of steps of the stairways are made of stone blocks in slight projection upon which have been sculpted saivite scenes: episodes depicting the deeds of Śiva or from the life of the Nāyanmārs. The same scenes may be depicted on a single block, or indeed comprise several episodes and cover seven, eight or ten blocks. These are roughly the same scenes which are found on the base of the inner gateway, and at Gangai in the vestibule on the western wall of the hall, facing the sanctum. The string walls of the stairways at Gangai are, on the other hand, entirely without sculpture.

Observing these three sites, one notes that the location of the scenes is different in them, that there is, therefore, no fixed sequence for the representations. As the sanctuary can be entered by the stairways in the east, south or north, no ambulatory direction is imposed. The images can be viewed independently of each other.

For each stairway, the string walls of the lower flight run along the top of the first base and those on the upper flight along the second base. There is, therefore, a slight difference in height between the two flights, but it is difficult to believe that for this reason the scenes of the lower flight are presented on a single tier, and those on the upper flight on two tiers.

Given below is the iconography of the stairways, as well as that of the inner gateway:

Scenes common to the stairway and the gateway	Tripurāntaka * Śiva's marriage * Kāmāntaka Caṇḍeśa * Pāśupatāstra * Bhikṣāṭana
Scenes only on the stairway	Gaṅgādhara Anugraha Dakṣari
Scenes only on the gateway	Kālāntaka * Kaṇṇappa * Subrahmaṇya Sundarar Gajāntaka Ardhanāri Pāṇḍavas

The scenes marked with an asterisk also appear in the vestibule at Gangai, with in addition Rāvaṇa shaking the Kailāsa and Viṣṇu Anugrahamūrti.

Southern Stairway, Eastern Face, Upper Flight

The whole flight is devoted to the story of Śiva Tripurāntaka depicted in a series of panels on two superposed tiers (Plate 9).

According to the myth, three demons obtained from Brahmā the possession of the three worlds. Only when the three cities (Tripura) become united every thousand years, can, with a single arrow, their destruction take place. But the demons will be protected if they worship Śiva. Annoyed by the comings and goings of the demons, the gods wish to destroy them. In an effort to do so, they cause malicious spirits to rise from a sacrifice and these attempt to destroy the Tripura demons, but without success because the latter are protected by their devotion to Śiva. However, offended at having been attacked, they torment the gods who then turn to Viṣṇu. The latter undertakes to divert the demons from their faith in Śiva which renders them invincible. Assuming the form of the Buddha, Viṣṇu incites the Tripura to follow his teaching and forsake Śiva. Mounted on his chariot, Śiva kills them with his arrow, with the exception of three of them who had remained faithful to him.

The myth undergoes a different iconographic translation in the three depictions of it in different places in the temple.

The painting on the northern wall of the circumambulatory corridor represents Śiva Tripurāntaka, with eight arms and holding weapons, mounted on his chariot and in the act of shooting an arrow at the Tripura demons and their consorts who, terrified, run in all directions. Deities on their mounts assist in the battle: Gaṇeśa, Subrahmaṇya, Durgā. In the upper portion of the painting is seen Viṣṇu as the Buddha (see Plate 16).

Entirely different is the representation on the inner gateway, for Śiva is not shown in the form of Tripurāntaka. On the upper tier, the Buddha is seated and encircled by Tripura demons listening to him, while the lower tiers are concerned with the debacle of the Tripura demons who fall to earth and flee. Śiva, unseen in the battle, only appears in the corner of the pavilion, seated on his throne beside Pārvāti and receiving the homage of the three Tripura demons. Yet again different is the representation on the string wall of the southern stairway. The Buddha, seated beneath the tree of enlightenment, is encircled by Tripura demons; on the adjacent panel, the same Buddha, still beneath the tree, but standing with upraised arm, probably in the act of preaching, is surrounded by Tripura demons who go over to him, their hands joined, standing or bowing. Following these two panels, which are viewed from left to right, the viewing should continue at the extreme right and once more proceed to the left. To the far right, then, only rough-hewn in the stone, six gods are standing and sending malefic spirits on the adjacent panel against the Tripura demons who are depicted on the next panel to the left. The malefic spirits, for the most part dwarves, bhūtas, are marching against the Tripura demons, their heads still turned towards the gods who have sent them into battle. The following panel, again to the left, is a scene of confusion in which some demons and their consorts face their adversaries, while others have already fallen to the ground, and yet others flee with their cattle in the opposite direction, carrying the liṅga of Śiva on their heads. In the midst of the demons, three edifices are represented which are certainly the three cities. One of them, of square plan, is crowned by a domed roof. The second edifice has a roof with either two or four slopes. Only the roof of the third can be seen, which is oblong in plan.

The upper tier is devoted to the surrender of the Tripura demons. On the panel to the left, several demons, holding liṅga in their hands or on their heads, advance towards Śiva, who is mounted on his chariot. Somewhat farther, to the right, three demons are in a row directly in front of Śiva's chariot, driven by Brahmā. Accompanied by two of his gnomes, Śiva is standing in the chariot, leaning on his bow, an arrow in the other hand. Behind the chariot is a new scene: Tripurāntaka is standing on the ground, beside him are three merely rough-hewn standing figures, probably gods, who are encouraging him to mount his battle chariot.

Southern Stairway, Eastern Face, Lower Flight (Plate 9)

The marriage of Śiva with Pārvatī is depicted on four panels. They are viewed from left to right, and on three panels are figures turned towards the fourth, which is depicting the marriage ceremony.

As in most representations of marriage, Pārvatī is to the right of Śiva, who takes her hand for the *"pāṇigrahaṇa"* rite, the "taking-the-hand" rite, before placing her on his left, the consort's customary place. At the feet of the future husband and wife, Brahmā is seated and officiates over the sacrificial fire. During the episode of the pillar of fire, he had obtained from Śiva the role of presiding deity at all sacrifices. He is nevertheless absent from the marriage scene of the inner gateway, where only Viṣṇu pours lustral water over the hands of the married couple. Here, recognizable because of his cylindrical tiara, he stands behind Brahmā. In fact, on other marriage representations the two deities participate in the celebration, Brahmā tending the sacrificial fire and Viṣṇu pouring the lustral water. The panel was not completed, but among the figures one nevertheless recognizes Nandikeśvara.

The three preceding panels depict in the foreground gaṇa musicians in the retinue of Śiva and, behind them, a sage and numerous two-armed male figures. It is probably Nārada and all the sons born of the mind and body of Brahmā. According to the *Śiva Purāṇa*, Śiva wished to have Brahmā, with his own escort, in his company when he visited his father-in-law (see also inner gateway Plate 13).

SOUTHERN STAIRWAY, WESTERN FACE, UPPER FLIGHT (Plate 10)

The lower tier of this flight includes only large stone blocks, in reserve, in abeyance, without sculptures.

On the upper level, one of the three panels is scarcely hewn and the deities are simply roughed out. One nevertheless recognizes that it is an "Anugrahamūrti", or "Śiva according his grace". The latter, with four arms, is seated near Pārvatī? and is leaning over to give with two hands an object to an unshaped mass, which must be a devotee. Two gandharvas are flying on the upper part of the panel and one gaṇa stands below.

The second panel is a representation of Gaṅgādhara. While the Gaṅgā descends from his hair, Śiva attempts to pacify Pārvatī who, jealous, turns away. On the side, Baghīrata is doing penance, arms upraised and supplicating Gaṅgā to descend to earth. Above is a small seated figure and below, near Pārvatī, a small naked female figure which cannot be identified. From the iconographic point of view, this representation of Śiva and Pārvatī in the form of Gaṅgādhara is similar to that found in the niches of temple façades. However, one recalls that in the northern niche at Tanjavur, Śiva Gaṅgādhara is without Pārvatī.

Kāmāntaka is on the third panel. Śiva is seated on Kailāsa, beside Pārvatī, encircled by flying gaṇa. Kāma, who Śiva has just struck down, is collapsing at his feet, supported by his consort Rati. This is only the central episode in the story of Kāma. It is more elaborate on the inner gateway, where Kāma shoots one of his arrows at Śiva, by whom he is subsequently struck down. Then, with joined hands, Kāma approaches the god who pardons him (see also Plate 14).

SOUTHERN STAIRWAY, WESTERN FACE, LOWER FLIGHT (Plate 10)

On the two panels on the left, deities are standing alongside each other, slightly turned toward the two other panels. One can identify Nandikeśvara, Nārada, Indra, Sūrya, Brahmā, Śiva beneath an umbrella and with Nandin at his side, Viṣṇu. The two remaining panels carry gaṇas, musicians and seven standing similar deities, heads encircled by an aureola, one hand in *abhaya*. This could represent the Indra's subterfuge and the story of the seven images of the nearby Tiruvarur temple.

Northern Stairway, Western Face, Upper Flight (Plate 11)

The story of Dakṣa is developed at length, covering the upper and lower flights. The lower tier of the upper flight represents the destruction of the sacrifice of Dakṣa. There follows the central scene, Śiva with four arms, an arrow in his hand, has decapitated Dakṣa. The latter's body lies on the ground in front of his weeping consort, whose arms are raised towards the heavens. Śiva, who has taken hold of Dakṣa's head by the hair, is in the act of putting it in the pit of the sacrificial fire, while a priest turns away. From the other side of this scene, a group of women and men watch as they move away in fright. The upper tier represents a succession of stately seated deities: Śiva, Pārvatī and the bull Nandin, to whom two sages are coming to render homage, then Viṣṇu and Brahmā.

Northern Stairway, Western Face, Lower Flight

On this flight Śiva is encircled by Brahmā and three sages. One can suppose that they have come to Śiva to request that he give Dakṣa a new head. On another panel one sees the latter with his ram's head, hands joined before Śiva, surrounded by rough-hewn figures, gaṇas and kinnara musicians.

Despite the popularity of this myth of Dakṣa among the Nāyanmārs, he was scarcely represented in sculpture. One of the rare known examples is at the Kailāsanātha in Kanchipuram, in which Śiva impales with his trident a double figure on the ground, Dakṣa and Yajña Puruṣa.

At the Tiruvalisvaram temple, dating from the tenth century, one of the stone reliefs in the tower represents Śiva standing with Pārvatī and, at the bottom of the relief, a gaṇa placing the head of a ram on the body of kneeling Dakṣa.

Northern Stairway, Eastern Face, Upper Flight (Plate 12)

The two tiers of this flight each depict an episode from saivite legend. On the upper flight is found the story of Caṇḍeśa, on the panels which are viewed from right to left.

The first panel contains two scenes which follow each other in time, but which interpenetrate and are laid out in tiers. On the side, Caṇḍeśa is worshipping in front of the liṅga, while above and in the centre his father approaches to take him by surprise. To the right, in the midst of a herd of cows, Caṇḍeśa brandishes a hatchet in front of his father who has already fallen to the ground. On the second panel, Śiva, seated on his throne at Pārvatī's side, is giving a garland to the kneeling Caṇḍeśa, whose hands are joined. Two standing figures, one hand raised, acclaim the event, just as six similar figures following them on the third panel are doing.

On the inner gateway, the story of Caṇḍeśa is told on superposed string-courses: below is a row of cows, while above, Caṇḍeśa is striking his father to the ground. Farther above, Śiva is seated on his throne; in front of him a figure has been clipped off, certainly Caṇḍeśa

(Plate 13).

The order of viewing of the four panels on the lower tier is from left to right, which is contrary to the order on the foregoing tier. To the left, on a long block of stone, are a few rough-hewn figures. The second panel shows Arjuna in a corner, arm upraised, doing penance to obtain the pāśupata weapon. Occupying an entire panel is the fight between Śiva and Arjuna as hunters, in the act of shooting arrows at each other. A dog, the dog of one of the hunters, crosses the scene. Near Arjuna is represented the boar which was the pretext of the confrontation between Śiva and Arjuna. On the third panel, Śiva and Pārvatī are seated on their thrones on Kailāsa, represented by a circumvolution of stones. Three figures are paying homage to them, their arms upraised, while seated at their feet, hands joined, Arjuna is receiving the pāśupata weapon from the hands of a gaṇa (see also inner gateway Plate 14).

On the fourth panel, several figures with raised hands salute the divine couple: a woman bearing a fly-whisk and men whose size progressively decreases follow the pitch of the wall.

NORTHERN STAIRWAY, EASTERN FACE, LOWER FLIGHT (Plate 12)

The entire flight with five panels is devoted to the representation of numerous women accompanied by two male figures. The first four panels show groups of five, four or three women, altogether fifteen, sometimes merely roughed out. They are standing side by side, naked, a lotus in the hand. Two male figures appear on the last panel. One of the two, apparently naked, hair falling to the shoulders, with two arms and holding an umbrella above his head could be Bhikṣāṭana, even though he does not have the characteristics usually ascribed to Bhikṣāṭana, and the women would then be the wives of the *ṛṣis* seduced by Bhikṣāṭana. The second bearded figure, with matted hair, portrays a sage holding a short staff.

This identification is, in fact, not satisfying and it appears that one would have to propose another, on the basis of the account of the Tripura demons as given in the *Liṅga Purana* and the *Śiva Purāṇa*. There it is said that the Puruṣa (Viṣṇu) deluded the daityas and that Nārada, the wielder of Māyā, deluded the women. The relief is not very clear and it could be that the male figure which appears to be naked is, in fact, clothed in a long robe clinging to the body like, in a more evident manner, the Buddha on the southern stairway who is alluring the Tripura demons. Similarly, the shoulder-length hair could rather be taken as short hair and distended earlobes, as befitting of the Buddha, and as is also evident for the same Buddha on the southern stairway. The umbrella over the head is, in addition, perfectly acceptable for a representation of the Buddha. The sage next to the Buddha, because of his position, is very possibly Nārada.

4. THE PILLARED HALL (Plates 7 & 8)

The question arises why there was such a large hall (later divided into two parts), and what was its purpose?

Orissa has kept a tradition of halls on the axis of the sanctuary, the name and function of which are well-known: *jagamohana* (audience hall), *naṭa maṇḍira* (dance hall), *bhoga maṇḍapa* (hall of enjoyment). There is, however, nothing so precise in the South, where primarily the *mukha maṇḍapa* (front hall) or the *maha maṇḍapa* (big hall) are known.

One of the first halls in the South is found at the Kailāsanātha in Kanchipuram. It is a small pillared pavilion, detached from the main shrine, and measures some ten metres on the side. Knowing that the goddess, in proximity of Śiva, is considered as *bhoga śakti*, the iconography on the outer walls of the pavilion, four goddesses (Lakṣmī, Sarasvatī, Durgā, Jyeṣṭhā), allow one to associate this pavilion with the *bhoga maṇḍapa* type. This tradition appears to be firmly established, as Sarasvatī and Lakṣmī are facing west' on the wall of the pillared hall, and because the same is the case for the hall in Gangai and the pavilions in front of the two Kailāsa at the same site. One also discovers that, despite disruptions, the same principle was at work in Darasuram on the wall of the façade of the inner hall and at Pavundarikapuram (Kumbakonam taluk).

However, one does not know exactly what a *bhoga maṇḍapa* was, and if it was not, in fact, a multi-purpose structure. It is, nevertheless, precluded that the pavilion of the Kailāsanātha had been intended for dance because of the smallness of its central space (1.20 m in length). On the other hand, it is not impossible that the big hall in Tanjavur had served as a dance hall. For one reason, the *devadāsī* system became increasingly widespread in that period, particularly in Orissa, and this was also the case in the South, as Rājarāja would have recruited four hundred dancers. The very nature of the hall (at least the western part near the sanctum) would lend itself to dance because of the free central space in the middle of the pillars. Moreover, it appears that there were only pillars and angle walls at each corner, creating a bright and ventilated construction.

Tanjavur seems to have been at a time during which ritual practices were undergoing radical change, for if the angle walls bore warriors, a little later in Gangai, it is musicians with *vīṇās* and cymbals *(tālas);* an appropriate iconography for a dance hall. The same is true for the pavilions of the two Kailāsa in Gangai. Finally, somewhat later, the hall with its pillars of concentric squares at Darasuram leaves a vast central space appropriate for the movements of dancers.

The hall at Tanjavur was definitely, among other things, intended for dance, even should the name *naṭa maṇḍapa* not be preserved to our days. However, according to *Tiruvisaippā* (eleventh century), beautiful young girls danced in the dance hall (*naṭaka śālai*) in front of the god Tañjai Rājarājeśvara. Was this *naṭaka śālai* the big hall, or was it a temporary pavilion in the temple courtyard? On the basis of inquiries made among former *devadāsīs*, one knows that their performance of ritual dance was not restricted to the presence of the principal deity, but that they also had to dance in front of certain subshrines, and above all in the courtyards of temples, or even outside on the occasion of festivals. Perhaps, when there came to be fewer dancers, and no longer the four hundred ones of Rājarāja, one stopped using the big hall for dance, and it was no longer necessary to refer to it as a dance hall. The hall was divided in two parts by a partition wall constituted of several reused stones bearing inscriptions from temples of an earlier date, and a small stele representing a dignitary whose clothing indicates the Nayak period. It could also be that because of this reorganization, the big hall was no longer considered as a dance hall and was therefore no longer referred to as such.

The iconography on the façades of this hall is concentrated on the corner angle walls in the east and west, and at the doorways. The eastern doorway, as well as that at the back of the hall opening onto the vestibule, is guarded by *dvārapāla* represented at an angle and with one leg crossed over the other, leaning on a heavy club standing next to the passage. They are four-armed and hold no attributes in their hands, in distinction to all the other *dvārapāla* of the sanctuary and vestibule.

The partition walls in the eastern part of the hall have together eight niches, four in the east, two in the south and two in the north. All the niches contain a standing warrior, sword and shield in hand. They are manifestly positioned there to defend the corners of the building (see Plates 7 & 8).

The back part of the hall does not have the same arrangement of eight niches, but only six, as a result of two small rooms with only doors for the entry of light located in the vestibule and concealing the wall where two niches should be found. Thus, two rather than four niches occupy the western façade, with Lakṣmī in the south and Sarasvatī in the north. The location of these goddesses is different from that of the foregoing pavilion, the sanctuary at the Kailāsanātha in Kanchipuram, where the north is reserved for the terrible or malefic goddesses Durgā and Jyeṣṭhā, and the south for the beneficent goddesses Lakṣmī and Sarasvatī. Similarly, Durgā faces the north and Lakṣmī faces south in the passage between the two courtyards of the Kailāsanātha.

In Tanjavur, and in Gangai where the same arrangement was adopted, the two goddesses are facing west and thus the deity of the sanctum. Lakṣmī is in the south and Sarasvatī in the north, perhaps because she is associated with Brahmā (Plates 7, 8).

Lakṣmī

The figures of Lakṣmī in the two temples have points in common. They are both seated in lotus position on a double-lotus pedestal, with inverted corolla, and have two hands and are holding opened lotuses. They also have the same conical hairstyle, the same breast band and the same double diagonal band. The decoration of the niches is, however, very different. In Gangai, the Lakṣmī is a Gajalakṣmī. The back of the niche is occupied by two elephants, drawn up in the act of pouring water over the goddess. In Tanjavur, in the niche the upper part of which is occupied by a tree, the goddess is beneath an umbrella and flanked by two gandharvas. On either side of her is a woman carrying a fly-whisk. The border of the niches is also very different in the two temples. In Tanjavur, there is a strict symmetry. On each side of the niche, two elephants sculpted in the plain wall recall that Lakṣmī is also Gajalakṣmī; above, four sages are seated and saluting the goddess, and at the very top are two flying gandharvas. In Gangai, the figures in the retinue are more numerous and the symmetry is less extensive: on the lower part, seated women are depicted; in the middle tier, women are holding fly whisks; and above, standing figures are saluting with one hand.

Sarasvatī

Sarasvatī is seated in lotus position beneath an umbrella surmounted by a tree which, certainly to denote that it is in the background, is very small. The goddess is flanked by two women bearing fly whisks; two gandharvas are flying around the tree. The goddess is wearing a breast-band and has two arms, one of which holds a book; the other, which is broken, must have held a water pot. She differs from the Sarasvatī in Gangai, whose breasts are bare and who has four arms, with rosary and water pot as attributes. In Tanjavur, Sarasvatī is surrounded by sages seated on either side of the niche; in Gangai, the retinue is more diverse, with animals, devotees and sages.

The same back part of the hall contains Gaṇapati and Viṣṇu in the south and Bhairava in the north. Gaṇapati and Durgā are customarily placed symmetrically to each other in sanctuary vestibules. Here, Viṣṇu is in symmetry with Durgā, his sister. The former must be present in a Śiva temple, but as all the statues of the sanctuary-tower are uniquely devoted to Śiva, Viṣṇu has been installed in the pillared hall.

Bhairava is in the north, as terrible forms of the deities generally are; he holds a skull and trident in his lower hands, and in his upper hands are bell and peacock feathers (Plate 7).

The four divine figures have a large retinue of devotees and sages sculpted in the protruding stone blocks on either side of the niches. The heads of three of them, Gaṇapati, Viṣṇu and Durgā, are in an aureola of flames similar to those found on bronze figures.

5. THE GALLERY AND ITS SUBSHRINES (Figure 4, p.23)

The enclosure wall of the temple is pierced by a gateway in the east, in addition to which are gates in the south, west and north. All are on the axis of the sanctum of the principal sanctuary, signifying that the deity radiates in the four directions. Independently of this symbolic function, the southern gate really does serve as a passage, perhaps for priests residing in the streets to the south of the temple, because for this gate the base of the gallery is cut by a passage on the level of the inner courtyard, which is not the case for the gates in the west and north.

The surrounding gallery built against the enclosure wall accommodates thirty-six subshrines which fall into two types: nine rectangular subshrines and twenty-seven square subshrines (two of which are included in the inner gateway). But, Gangai possesses thirty-two subshrines. What is the reason for this difference?

As a general rule, the deities in Śiva's retinue are arranged all around the principal sanctuary in the temple courtyard, and one knows more or less what a divine court of eight deities is, despite the variations in text and reality. As for larger numbers of divine attendants, which are common in texts concerning temples, they only appear to exist at the Kailāsa in Kanchipuram, as well as in Tanjavur and Gangai.

According to texts dealing with ritual, the courtyards of temples correspond to diagrams divided into a specific number of squares, some of which are reserved for deities. The simplest case is that of a diagram with nine squares and eight attendant deities, while the central square is reserved for the principal deity.

There are, for example:

The diagram with 25 squares and 12 deities;

the diagram with 36 squares and 16 deities; and

the diagram with 49 squares and 32 deities.

In the latter case, according to information in the *Mayamata,* the thirty-two deities are arranged in the courtyard of the temple in two concentric squares, which is not the case in Gangai.

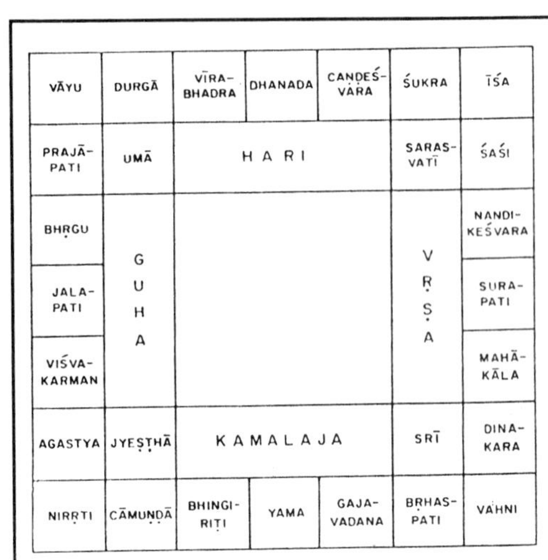

Figure 3. Śiva's retinue according to *Mayamata* (from Dagens, 1970)

The *Dīptāgama* and the *Ajitāgama* also foresee

thirty-two deities, but they are distributed in the outer (fourth) square; the third square contains sixteen deities, the second eight deities, and the first, near the sanctuary, is occupied by Caṇḍikeśvara. The total number given in the *Kāmikāgama* is larger and the thirty-two deities are in the fifth square.

The thirty-two subshrines are evidently related to the thirty-two deities in the texts mentioned above. Nevertheless, Gangai has no concentric squares with eight and sixteen deities (or, according to the *Kāmikāgama,* with 8, 12, 24 deities).

As for Tanjavur, there are no references for the thirty-six subshrines, because that number of deities is not given in the texts. On the other hand, there is a diagram with thirty-six squares (and 16 deities). Would there have been confusion on the part of the builders between the number of squares and the number of deities?

Among the thirty-six subshrines at Tanjavur, one may assume that the square subshrines were intended for a single deity and that those of rectangular plan were for a group of deities. The nine Āditya found in Gangai allow of this type of reconstruction, just as in Tanjavur the presence of a Chola Vārāhī in the courtyard leads one to think that the Seven Mothers were accommodated in a rectangular shrine.

The disposition of subshrines does not correspond to a principle of symmetry; there is not the same number of subshrines in the south as in the north, nor in the east as in the west. Furthermore, a rectangular subshrine does not correspond to a rectangular subshrine facing it.

Of the thirty-six subshrines, thirteen are identifiable with certainty because the statue is in place, or because an element enables one to establish which deity occupied it (Plate 17). There are, first:-

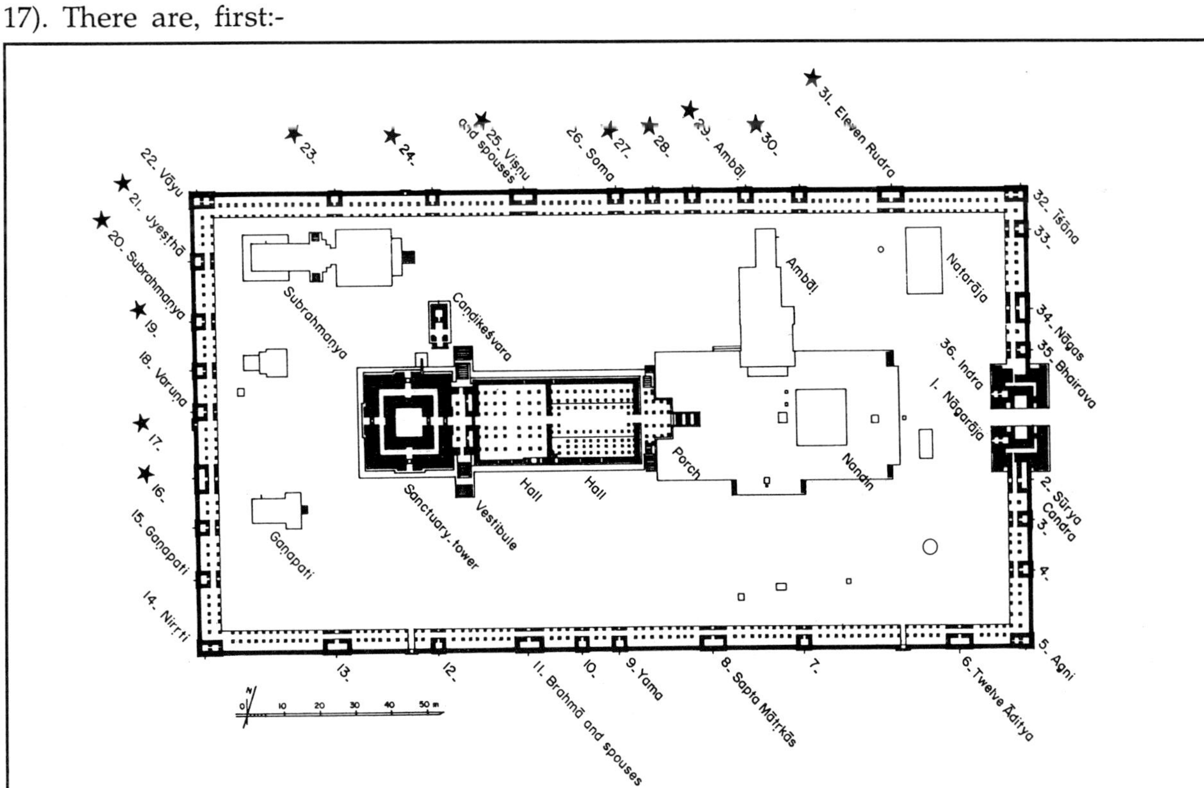

Figure 4. The subshrines of the gallery (*subshrines containing a liṅga)

Nāgarāja, height 190 cm, subshrine 1. Seated, with two arms. The presence of a naga appears to have been prevalent during the Chola period; several of them have been found in Gangai and one appears in a niche of the Darasuram temple.

Agni, height 190 cm, subshrine 5. Seated, encircled by an aureola of flames, the crossed legs are held by a yoga belt. He has a long beard and flaming hair. The left hand holds a water pot and the right, which is broken, probably held a rosary, like the Agni of the Chola statue in the Tanjavur museum, with whom this Agni has the yoga belt in common.

The Seven Mothers, subshrine 8. A mutilated Vārāhī in Chola style is found in the courtyard near subshrine 8. The dimensions of what remains (102 cm) allow one to say that the rectangular subshrine 8 accommodated the group comprising the Seven Mothers.

Yama, subshrine 9. Yama's mount, the buffalo, is present in the four corners of the roof.

Nirṛti, subshrine 14. The human mount of this deity is present.

Gaṇapati, height 162 cm, subshrine 15.

Varuṇa, height 165 cm, subshrine 18. This statue is in place and there are sea monsters on the roof. The two-armed god is holding appropriately the noose; the other hand makes the gesture of fearlessness.

Vāyu, height 175 cm, subshrine 22. The four arms of the deity are broken. The god's mount, the antelope, is seen near the roof.

Soma, subshrine 26. According to ancient tradition, in the *Atharvaveda*, the north was devoted to Soma, who was then progressively replaced by Kubera. The summit of the subshrine bears a lion in each of the four corners. The lion is not the customary mount of either Soma or Kubera, except in the *Matsya Pūraṇa* where it is attributed to Soma. Moreover, one observes that the octagonal drum beneath the roof bears a small figure on four sides. Quite eroded, the figure is standing, arms crossed at chest level, in the same posture as Candra holding two lotuses. The subshrine was therefore certainly dedicated to Soma. It is known, however, that Kubera was more common, as the outer gateway at Darasuram shows. There, among the eight Directions, appears if not his statue, at least an inscription naming him.

Ambāl, subshrine 29. An inscription on the pillar of the gallery facing the subshrine mentions a gift made to the sanctuary *(alaiyani)* of Umāparameśvari.[7]

Īśāna, height 185 cm, subshrine 32. The arms are broken.

Bhairava, subshrine 35. Bhairava's place is to the right of the entrance to the temple. Did the subshrine once contain the eight-armed Bhairava which is now beneath the porch? This is doubtful because his size (133 cm) does not correspond to the dimensions of the Directions, which are still in place and are much larger.

Indra, subshrine 36. On the drum of the superstructure of this subshrine is found a sculpture of Indra, thunderbolt in hand.

The occupants of the other subshrines can be identified with reasonable certainty. They are: *Sūrya* and *Candra,* subshrine 2.

Twelve Āditya, rectangular subshrine 6, in the south, as in the Kailāsanātha in Kanchipuram. *Brahmā* and his two consorts, subshrine 11 in the south and, opposite to them in the north, *Viṣṇu* and his consorts, subshrine 25. At the Kailāsa, these two deities are symmetrically disposed on the level of the sanctum of the sanctuary.

Subrahmaṇya, subshrine 20.

Jyeṣṭhā, subshrine 21.

Eleven Rudra, rectangular subshrine 31, in the north as at the Kailāsanātha.

Several *Nāgas,* rectangular subshrine 34.

Thus, twenty-one of the total of thirty-six subshrines can be considered as identified. Thirteen subshrines contain at present a liṅga, but it is not certain that this was originally foreseen, as two specific cases show. Subshrines 20 and 29 each contain a liṅga, while 20 could only have been dedicated to Subrahmaṇya and 29 to Ambāl.

On the other hand, apart from the subshrines, the western gallery contains 108 liṅga which were installed at the beginning of the nineteenth century by King Serfoji. They came from the temple of thousand liṅga *(āyirattali)* in Nandipuram (now Virasingapettai, about eight kilometres north of Tanjavur).[8] These are votive liṅga, like the 108 at the Papanasam temple which, according to legend, Rāma and Sītā installed to expiate the sin of killing Rāvaṇa. It is very possible that the votive liṅga were put in subshrines which had become empty.

6. THE INNER GATEWAY

The two gateways differ radically from the earlier small gateways (Kanchipuram, Kilaiyur-Melappaluvur), as from the larger gateways of the twelfth and thirteenth centuries. They introduce what will become general practice: an outer gateway of greater height than the inner gateway.

The two gateways in Tanjavur have an outer façade different from the inner façade, a feature not found among later gateways. The inner façade opening onto the courtyard contains, on either side of the axial passage, two small shrines which belong to the series of thirty-six subshrines of the gallery.

Whereas the outer gateway is devoid of iconography (with the exception of the superstructure covered with stucco figures), low reliefs are arrayed on the base of the inner gateway. The main body bears figures in high relief.

The base rests on a plinth and is crowned with a small cornice. It is divided by pilasters into panels each depicting a saivite scene; the panel itself is divided into four strips one above the other. As is the case regarding the iconography of the stairway of the main shrine, it is difficult to detect a veritable iconographic programme. While several representations are current and are found on the stairways and on the wall of the vestibule in Gangai, a few scenes are extremely rare, like the episode of Subrahmaṇya and Vaḷḷi, or the depiction of the Pāṇḍavas before Indra.

Base, Outer Face, Right Side (Plate 13)

First panel

The panel begins, on the upper strip, with a representation of a devotee, hands joined. It continues below, with Subrahmaṇya, identifiable by his conical crown and double chest-band;

nearby a goddess, probably Devasenā, is seated beneath an umbrella. The next strip shows the four-armed Subrahmaṇya, holding two thunderbolts; he is flanked by his two consorts, Vaḷḷi and Devasenā. His peacock stands on the small lower strip.

This is the first time that Subrahmaṇya appears on the right side of an entrance. It becomes customary, beginning in the Chola period, to find Gaṇapati to the left of the entrance to a gateway or shrine, and Subrahmaṇya to the right.

Second panel

Here, the episode in which Vaḷḷi is seduced by Subrahmaṇya is depicted. Subrahmaṇya, in the form of a hunter, pays court to Vaḷḷi as she guards the millet field of her father, Nampi, who is a hunter. When the latter appears bearing food for his daughter, Subrahmaṇya immediately transforms himself into a tree. Once Nampi has left, Subrahmaṇya again assumes human form and urges Vaḷḷi to become his wife. Again, the father arrives, now accompanied by other hunters. This time Subrahmaṇya assumes the form of a very old saivite devotee and asks Vaḷḷi for food and water. She appeases his hunger and thirst, but he desires that she also soothe his feverish love. Frightened by this declaration, Vaḷḷi flees, whereupon Subrahmaṇya causes an elephant to appear in her path. Terrified, she turns back, running to the old man (Subrahmaṇya) and asking him for help. The latter removes the elephant, then leads Vaḷḷi into a grove where he embraces her. It is then that he reveals his godly form, seated on his peacock. Vaḷḷi prostrates herself at his feet and Subrahmaṇya lifts her up, promising to rejoin her later. The panel narrates only part of the story. On the upper strip, the old man beneath his umbrella approaches Vaḷḷi, who is seated in the millet field. The elephant appears on the second strip, at the same time as the manifestation of Subrahmaṇya. Curiously, on the third strip Subrahmaṇya, who is mounted on the elephant he caused to appear, is moving away from Vaḷḷi, whose arms are raised in salutation. The last strip depicts hunters from Vaḷḷi's tribe.

Third panel

This is a large scene which, contrary to the preceding one, is viewed upwards from the bottom. The lower strip, consisting of gaṇas and wild animals, depicts a forest landscape. Above, Arjuna does penance to obtain the pāśupata weapon. Immediately following, the combat with bows between Arjuna and Śiva unfolds; Pārvatī is present with the child Skanda on her hip. The strip continues with a row of six gods. On the strip above, Śiva and Pārvatī, bow in hand, are underway to Kailāsa. Near them a gaṇa gives the personified weapon, pāśupatāstra, to Arjuna, who is standing with joined hands. Male figures in a row salute the event. The uppermost strip portrays other male figures, seated sages and gandharvas acclaiming the bestowal of the weapon.

The entire panel bears numerous gods or male figures in the act of saluting, a way to fill this large panel (compare the same episode on the northern stairway of the main shrine).

Fourth panel

Two gods are seen between the upper strip with its gandharvas and the gaṇas on the lower strip. Above, near a gandharva symbolizing the heavens, Indra is on his throne, one hand forming the gesture of fearlessness. Below, he is apparently interceding with Brahmā, who is seated with his consort standing at his side.

Fifth panel

Between the upper and lower strips depicting gaṇas, the five Pāṇḍavas are seen walking towards the strip below, where Indra and his consort are seated, encircled by women holding fly- whisks.

Sixth panel

The upper strip portrays seated sages; below, Kāma is shooting an arrow at Śiva, seated on Kailāsa. Farther below, Kāma falls before his spouse, his arms raised in despair. Beside them, Kāma and his spouse are shown rendering homage to Śiva, seated on his throne, who has pardoned Kāma. The last strip consists of a row of gaṇas.

Seventh panel

Two strips on this panel depict seated sages; below is a strip with gaṇas.

Eighth and Ninth panels

These panels are located at the corner of the gateway, facing north. They are smaller than the previous panels and have only three strips. The two panels devoted to Kaṇṇappa, the hunter should be viewed together. On the lower strip, dogs are seen, as appropriate for hunters. Above, Kaṇṇappa, bow in hand, is walking; immediately following is a scene in which he is venerating a liṅga beneath a tree. Somewhat farther, he is kneeling near the liṅga, no doubt ready to offer his second eye, for an arm appears from the liṅga to prevent him from doing so. Kaṇṇappa is standing on the last and upper strip, his hands folded, offering worship in front of Śiva's shrine. One can assume that he has reached Śiva's paradise, for gandharvas are flying on either side.

Among the sixty-three Nāyanmār, only three of them are representated: Caṇḍeśa, Sundarar and Kaṇṇappa (who is also on one of the dormer-windows on the cornice of the main shrine (Plate 18). This hunter-devotee of Śiva was highly venerated as is revealed by several bronzes of him and by one inscription of Tiruvalanjuli (Kumbakonam taluk) dated from Rājarāja II. It records a gift of land to meet the expenses for the worship of Kaṇṇappa, and for two of the most famous Nāyanmār, Sundarar and Māṇikkavāsagar.[9] Kaṇṇappa is also abundantly featured on small panels in temples built before or after Tanjavur.

OUTER FACE, LEFT SIDE (Plate 14)

First panel

This narrow panel has three strips, on each of which is portrayed a two-armed male figure difficult to identify.

Second panel

Mārkaṇḍeya's story is illustrated on three strips. On the uppermost, Yama is shown running after Mārkaṇḍeya, who clings to the liṅga. Below, Śiva, trident in hand, has just struck Yama, who is falling. Then, on the lower strip, Mārkaṇḍeya is kneeling, offering thanks to the liṅga.

Third panel

The upper two strips depict sages and flying gandharvas; beneath this, the marriage of Śiva is represented. Pārvatī and her female attendants are to the left of Śiva, who takes her by the hand while Viṣṇu prepares to pour lustral water over the couple. A retinue of figures, hands joined, attend the ceremony. The lower strip portrays gaṇas playing music.

Fourth panel

The story of Caṇḍeśa is told. The episode is viewed from the bottom upwards. The lower strip depicts cows which are being watched over by Caṇḍeśa. On the next strip, near the liṅga of sand made by him beneath a tree, Caṇḍeśa, arms raised, has struck his father, who has fallen to the ground. On the upper strip, not the customary crowning of Caṇḍeśa by Śiva and Pārvatī is seen, but Śiva alone as Caṇḍeśa stands before him (compare with the northern stairway, Plate 12).

Fifth panel

This panel has been chipped off and is difficult to read. It is apparently to be viewed from the bottom upwards. Following a row of gaṇas, a strip shows Viṣṇu and Śiva seated, flanked by two doorkeepers (*dvārapāla*). Above, a male figure is kneeling before a standing god. On the uppermost strip, figures are standing in a row in front of a god seated with his consort.

Sixth panel

This panel is also quite damaged. Other than gaṇas and utensils for worship, such as pots and lamps, on the lower strip, only Śiva is shown, emerging from the pillar of fire (Liṅgodbhavamūrti) on one of the median strips.

Seventh panel

At the top, Śiva Candraśekhara is standing; the axe is visible in one of his four hands. Below are two standing male figures.

Eighth and Ninth panels

Located at the corner of the gateway, facing south, the panels with only three strips have been almost entirely chipped off. King Cēramān Perumān on his horse and Sundarar on an elephant are moving towards Kailaśa, where Śiva and Pārvatī are seated. The upper strip contains a row of gods, probably Śiva's attendants on Kailāsa.

INNER FACE, RIGHT SIDE (Plate 16)

This façade, which is quite damaged, appears to be devoted solely to the story of Tripurāntaka, despite being divided into panels.

First panel

The three strips show gods walking to the right, towards the next panel. Only Brahmā is recognizable.

Second panel

As on the preceding panel, gods and warriors are walking again to the right. Yama is on his buffalo, Gaṇapati on his rat and Subrahmaṇya is seated on his peacock. On the painting in the corridor of the sanctuary-tower, the same deities participate in the fight.

Third panel

On the upper strip, the Buddha is seated beneath a tree and is encircled by figures, the Tripura demons, who are paying homage to him. The two strips below represent figures who have fallen to the ground or are fleeing, carrying liṅgas on their heads and in their hands, the Tripura demons vanquished by Tripurāntaka. The latter, however, does not appear anywhere on the façade (compare with the southern stairway, Plate 9).

Fourth panel

It consists of two strips portraying Tripura women as they walk. One Tripura leads one of them by the hand.

Fifth and Sixth panels

These are located at the corner of the gateway, facing north. Śiva, mounted on his bull, holding the kettledrum and the snake, appears before four wives of the Tripura. The god is encircled by gaṇa musicians and figures carrying umbrellas. The lower, unfinished, strip appears to represent Śiva and Pārvatī on Kailāsa, encircled by gaṇas; in front of them three men worship the divine couple, the Tripuras. On the sixth panel, also incomplete, one distinguishes two standing four-armed gods.

INNER FACE, LEFT SIDE (Plate 15)

This façade was never completed. There are no scenes on strips, but only three large gods, each occupying an entire panel. The first panel represents Śiva Candraśekhara, whose axe is discernable. The second shows Gajasaṃhāramūrti, and in the third, Bhikṣāṭana is encircled by wives of the *ṛṣis*. The fourth, fifth and sixth panels consist only of protruding, uncarved stones.

THE MAIN BODY

In the east, above the base on either side of the axial passage, the main body has two symmetrical, imposingly large door-keepers. They are four-armed and making gestures befitting of *dvārapālas*, one foot resting on their clubs.

The extremities of the main body are provided with niches containing Sūrya in the south and Candra in the north. Only Sūrya has an elongated aureola behind his head. He has one hand on his hip and holds with the other an open lotus. Candra, in the same pose, holds a closed lotus (Plate 14).

7. THE SUBSIDIARY SHRINES IN THE COURTYARD (Figure 4, p. 23)

CAṆḌIKÉŚVARA SHRINE

The subshrine dedicated to Caṇḍikésvara was built at the same time as the main shrine. Like the one in Gangai it is much bigger than the Caṇḍikésvara shrines in other temples. Although it shelters Caṇḍeśa, who is meant to drink the sacred water discharged from the cella, it is not in front of the sprout emerging from the cella. It stands at the north-eastern corner of the sanctuary-tower, as is the case for all other Caṇḍikésvara shrines. This means that Caṇḍikésvara is identified with Śiva, and for this reason is located in the Śiva-Īśa corner, the north-east. Moreover, it appears that Caṇḍikésvara has been gradually considered as the guardian of Śiva's possessions, to the detriment of Bhairava-Kṣetrapāla at the entrance of the temple complexes. After circumambulating Śiva's shrine, the devotee is supposed to testify that he does not carry away the possessions of the god. This is the reason why Caṇḍikeśvara stands in the north-eastern corner, which is the end of the circumambulatory circuit around the sanctuary-tower, and at the same time the proximity of the holy water coming out of the cella. In the temples facing west, the circumambulation is done as for the temples facing east, even though Caṇḍikeśvara is standing on the north-western corner, the beginning of the circuit. In this case, obviously, the importance is given to the proximity of the ablution water channel.

The Caṇḍikeśvara shrine of Tanjavur consists of a square cella, preceded by an open forepart resting on two angle walls. The three façades of the sanctum have a niche, each with the same figure of a standing Caṇḍikeśvara with the left hand resting on the hip and the second one holding the axe. The cella does not contain the original Chola sculpture as in Gangai, (Plate 18) but has a small sitting figure from a later period. In both cases Caṇḍikésvara holds the axe. According to the story, Caṇḍeśa hit his fater's leg with a rod. But in iconography, he carries either the rod/club or the axe. This latter attribute, frequently in his hands, confirms his identification with Śiva.

GAṆAPATI SHRINE

It is a nineteenth century shrine, in the south-western corner of the courtyard, duplicating the nearby Gaṇapati's subshrine of the gallery which belongs to the original programme of the temple complex. The sanctum, with empty niches, is preceded by a closed forepart and a pillared hall, added at a later date. The cella contains a four-armed sitting Gaṇapati.

KARUVŪR DĒVAR SHRINE

This small late nineteenth century shrine is built at the back of the courtyard, almost facing the Chola painting in the corridor of the sanctuary-tower which represents Rājarāja and his guru Karuvūr Dēvar. This kind of shrine, which has no agamic sanction, was probably erected through the initiative of influential local devotees, with the approval of temple authorities. The sage has the same iconographic features as the late bronze of Karur (Karuvūr) city. He has a sage's headdress and a beard, and is seated cross-legged, his two hands on his knees hanging open, with one rosary around each thumb.

The shrine is heavily attended by the devotees, especially on Thursdays, as, apart from being the guru of the king and the author of *Tiruvisaippā*, Karuvūr Dēvar has been elevated to the status of a saint with the powers of a *siddha*. His worship is more or less combined with the one of the nearby married trees.

SUBRAHMAṆYA SHRINE

This shrine is in the north-western corner of the courtyard. Normally the centre shrine in the west is meant for Subrahmaṇya and the north-western for Jyeṣṭhā, but when the worship of Jyeṣṭha declined, the north-western corner was generally attributed to Subrahmaṇya as is the case here.

The shrine was built by the Nayaks in the seventeenth century and a pillared hall was added shortly after. During the Maratha period (eighteenth-nineteenth centuries), this hall was closed by walls to accommodate large portrait paintings of the Maratha rulers of the region. The sanctum, the vestibule and the forepart have one niche on each of their façades. The ones of the sanctum shelter have three identical four-armed Subrahmaṇya standing with the peacock behind him. He carries in his upper hands his two common varieties of thunderbolt. The niches of the vestibule are occupied by claustra. As for the forepart, it is the usual iconographic scheme for saivite temples, whether they are dedicated to the goddess or to Subrahmaṇya: the southern niche is for Gaṇapati and the northern one for Durgā. Apart from these high-relief figures, the walls have several small intricate and delicate sculptures. The main deity in the cella is a six-headed Subrahmaṇya with his peacock, flanked by his two spouses.

AMMAN SHRINE

This thirteenth century shrine in the north-eastern quarter of the courtyard has obviously been built to replace the Chola goddess subshrine in the gallery, just at the back. As it is normal for the early goddess shrines, it faces south, and is not parallel to Śiva's shrine, a more common feature during the subsequent periods. It consists of a square cella, also an early feature compared to the later rectangular cellae. The cella is preceded by a long vestibule, a closed pillared hall and a later period large pillared hall with a small porch. The niches of the sanctum and of the vestibule are now empty except for one. Normally it is common to find in them Gaṇapati and six different forms of the goddess with an iconography akin to the one of the Sapta Mātṛkās. The sides of the closed hall leading to the cella are occupied by large painted stucco panels devoted to the adoration of the liṅga. On one of them, Mārkaṇḍeya clings to the liṅga while Śiva emerges from it to fight Kāla; in front of it, Vyāghrapāda worships the liṅga from the top of a tree. Close to the vestibule, on one panel, Pārvatī surrounded by her followers is seated worshipping the liṅga, while on the opposite panel she is embracing the liṅga. The ceiling of the large hall is covered by paintings in narrow strips narrating the various fights of the goddess against the asuras.

In the cella, the consort of Śiva, Bṛhanāyakī, is a seventeenth century sculpture. She is standing, with four hands, one in *abhaya* and the other one in *varada*, the upper hands hold the rosary and the lotus, two very common attributes for the goddess in the Kaveri delta region.

CONCLUSION

The Bṛhadīśvara is a case of art closely connected with royal patronage. Thanks to the will of Rājarāja and large amounts of land and money, the temple was conceived as a unit, built in a single endeavour, on an exceptional scale. Doubtlessly, as it does not follow conventional size, careful architectural planning was done, certainly under the supervision of the king himself. It is an experiment never tried before, and attempted only once later, at Gangai. As for the iconography, the most original feature, never emulated elsewhere in the same way, is the sculptural rendering of two intertwined concepts : the *pañca brahmā* and the *parāmananda tāṇḍava*, a specific ruling on the subject laid down by theologians of the royal entourage, in concert with the builders of the monument.

The royal presence was made visible through the choice of Tripurāntaka as a leitmotif linking the god and the ruler, and the insistence on the representation of the battle against the Tripura demons (on the painting and the bas-reliefs), testifies to the fact that the religious confrontations were mainly under royal patronage. The importance of the Tripurāntaka motive, in relation with royalty, did not fail to attract Rājarāja II who developed it emphatically at Darasuram.

Another type of innovation is the architectural-iconographical vase-pilaster, unknown in Tamilnadu before Tanjavur, a bold re-creation from an old motive which became the norm for the following centuries.

Apart from these original creations, for the iconography in the niches of the main shrine, of the stairways and the inner gateway, it appears that the sculptors were free in their choice of figures and that they drew from a catalogue of forms known to them at that time. A prevailing convention was followed without looking for any innovative sculptural programme that the large scale of the temple would have permitted. There are several repetitive figures, especially in the arcatures or in the blind dormer-windows, but none of the themes—uncommon to Tamilnadu, however well-known they might have been—like Śiva slaying the demon Andhaka, Śiva and Pārvatī gambling at dice, Rāvaṇa shaking mount Kailāsa nor any representation of the *Mahābhārata* and the *Rāmāyaṇa* were chosen, however rich in narratives they could have been.

From the Puranic scenes on the stairways and the inner gateway, it is evident that the layout and the nature of the reliefs are not related. Moreover, for the niches of the main shrine, there is no evidence of any specific thematic linkages or of any hierarchic order of ascendoncy. In short, no veritably conceived iconographic programme. Some sculptures on the sanctuary-tower, on the gateway or on the stairways were never finished for whatever reason. This shows that the work was entrusted to different, separate teams of sculptors, having their own sculptural iconic store of knowledge.

But this does not mean that there was no scheme at all, and the presence of the goddesses on the main shrine is a case in point in this respect. From the Pallava conception of four goddesses on a pavilion in front of the main shrine, Tanjavur set the trend for the new principle of having two goddesses, Lakṣmī and Sarasvatī, symmetrically placed in the niches of the hall, facing the god. This formula was adopted by Gangai, Darasuram, Tribhuvanam and Pavundarikapuram (Kumbakonam taluk) with the two goddesses on the hall of the main shrine, facing either east or west. But roughly one century after Tanjavur, temples evolved also their own scheme as the twin representation of Nandikeśvara and Kaṇṇappa in symmetrical niches in front of the main shrine, at Darasuram, Pavundarikapuram, Korukkai (Kumbakonam taluk), Achyutamangalam (Nannilam taluk).

REFERENCES

1. Héléne Brunner, L'image divine dans le culte āgamique de Śiva, *L'image divine, cults et méditation dans l'Hindouisme,* Editions du CNRS, Paris, 1990,
2. *South Indian Inscriptions,* vol. II, part 2, Insc. 30, pp. 137-38.
3. A. Ekambaranathan, The Concept of Tripurāntaka and Rājarāja I, *Tamil Civilization,* vol. 3, no 2-3, Thanjavur, 1985, pp. 112-15. Gary J. Schwindler, Speculations on the theme of Śiva as Tripurāntaka as it appears during the reign of Rājarāja I in the Tanjore area ca. A.D. 1000, *Ars Orientalis* 17, 1987, pp. 163-78. D. Dayalan, Hymns of Nayanmars and the Tripurāntaka Episode in Big Temple, Thanjavur, *Indian Archaeological Heritage, Shri K. V. Soundara Rajan Festschrift,* vol. I, Delhi, Agam Kala Prakashan , 1991, pp. 445-47. Gerd J. R. Mevissen, The suggestion of movement: a contribution to the study of chariot-shaped structures in Indian temple-architecture, *Explorations in Art and Archaeology of South Asia: Essays dedicated to N.G. Majumdar,* ed. by Debala Mitra, Calcutta, Directorate of Archaeology and Museums, 1996, pp. 477-512.
4. R. Nagaswamy, New Light on Mamallapuram, *Transactions of the Archaeological Society of South India for the period 1960-62, Silver Jubilee Volume,* Madras, 1962, Appendix 4, pp. 35-41.
5. The gateways of Chidambaram temple have several representations of the sixteen-armed fighting goddess, Mahiṣāsuramardinī. But according to one inscription under one of the four goddesses, she is called Tripurasundarī.
6. J.M. Somasundaram Pillai, *The Great Temple at Tanjore,* Tanjore Palace Devasthanams, 1958, p. 36.
7. Information R. Nagaswamy.
8. Kudavayil Balasubrahmanyam, *Nandipuram,* INTACH Publications, Chennai, 1992, p. 70.
9. *Annual Report on Indian Epigraphy* for the year 1903, p. 19.

List of Plates

PLATES

Plate 1. Bṛhadīśvara temple

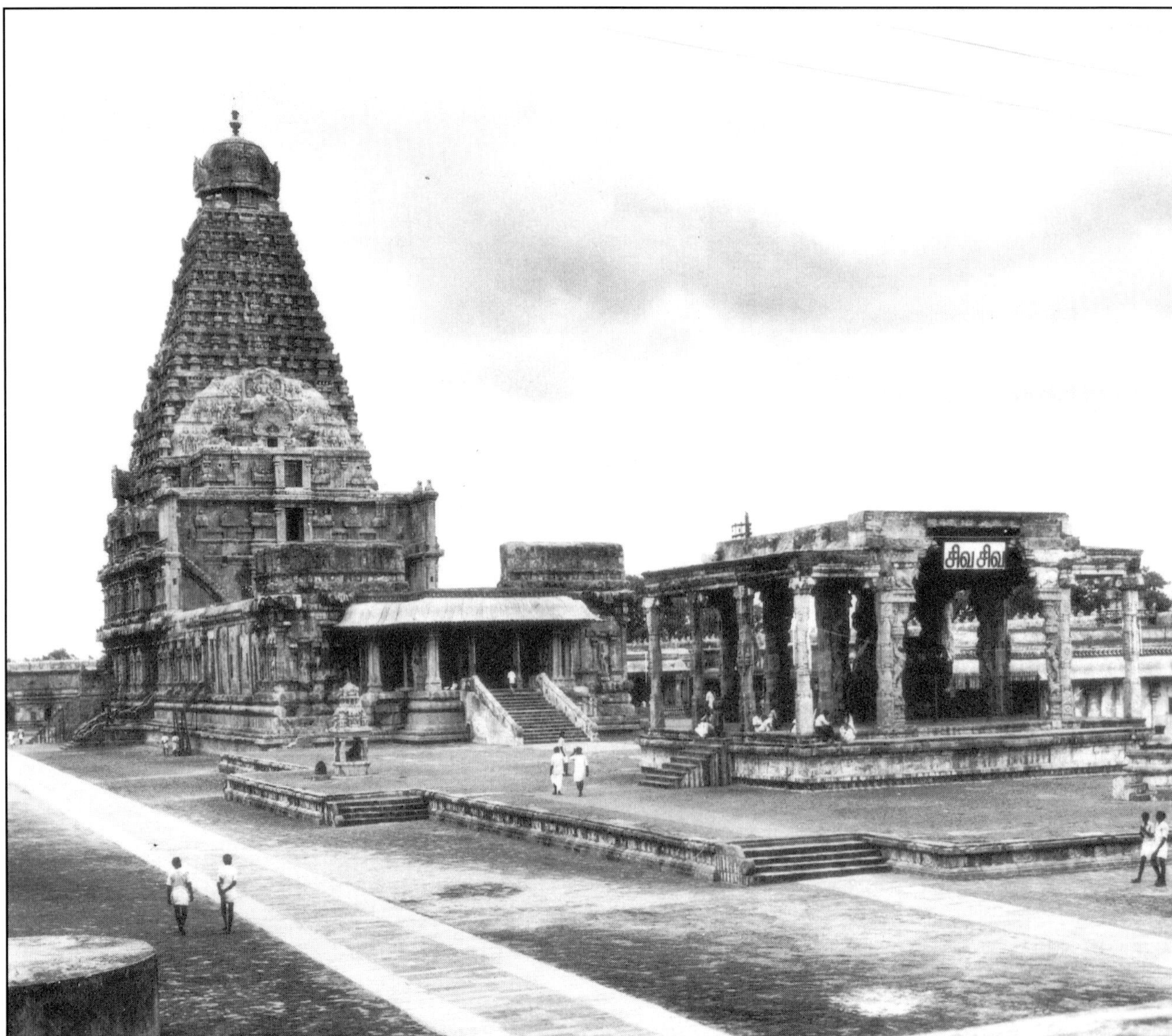

The main shrine from the South-East

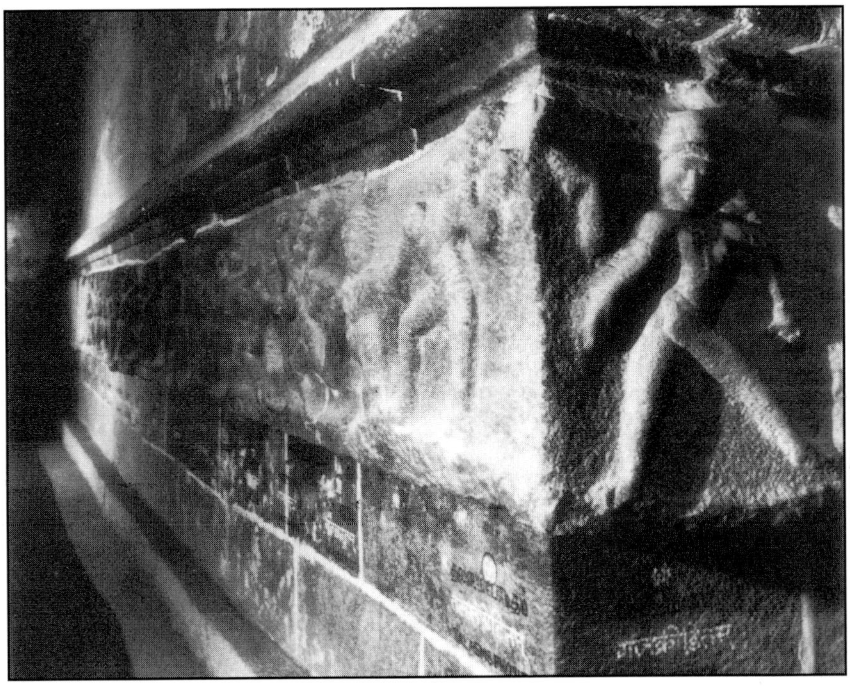

Circumambulatory corridor of the upper floor

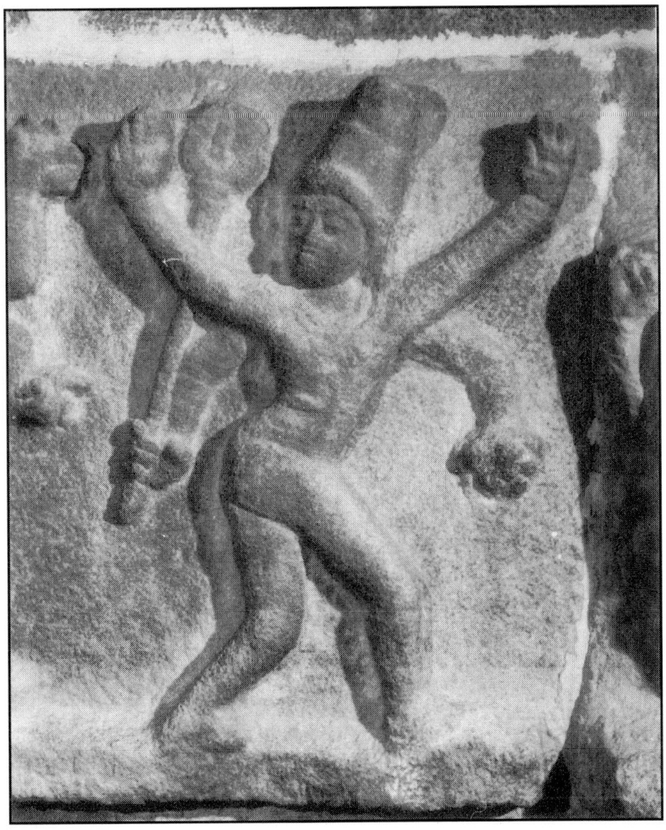

Dance pose in the corridor

Plate 2. Sanctuary-tower, iconography of the ground floor

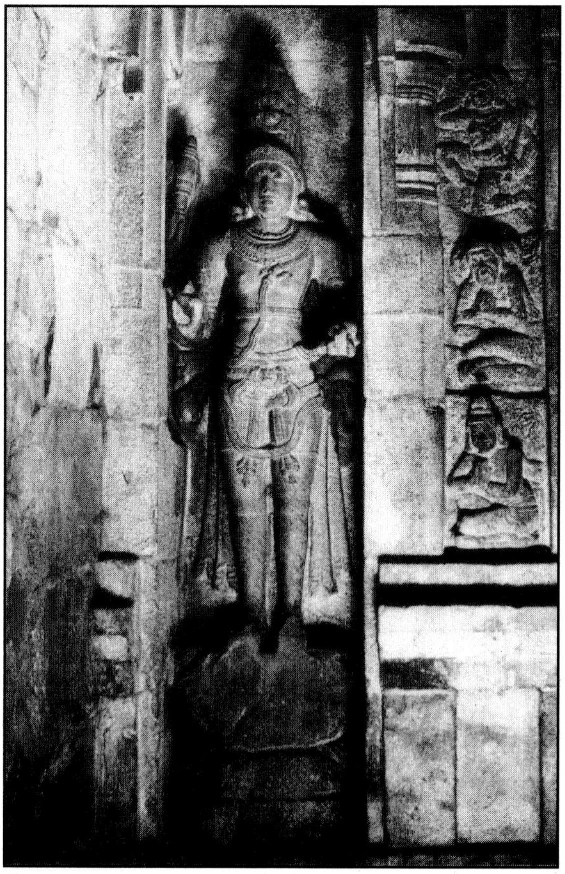

Śiva

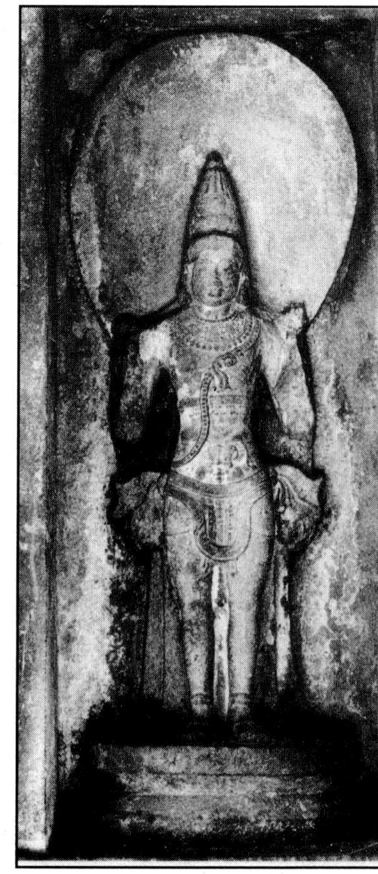

Sūrya

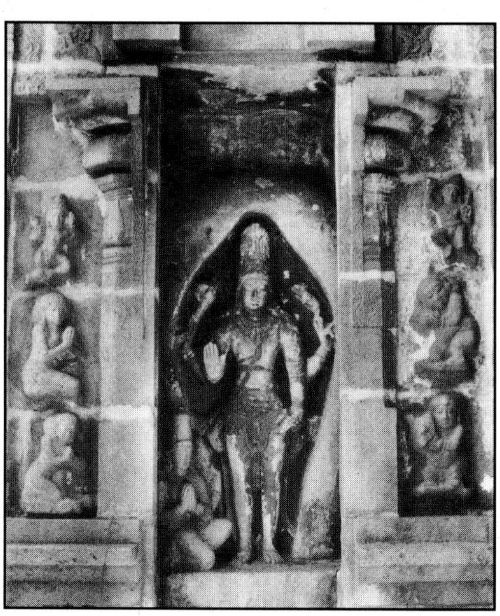

Liṅgodbhavamūrti

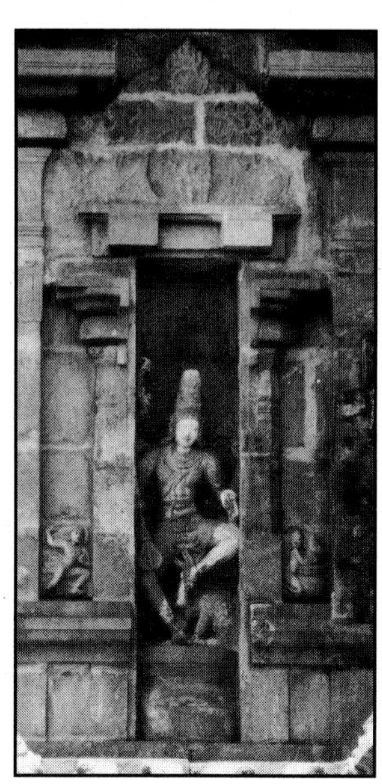

Kalāntaka

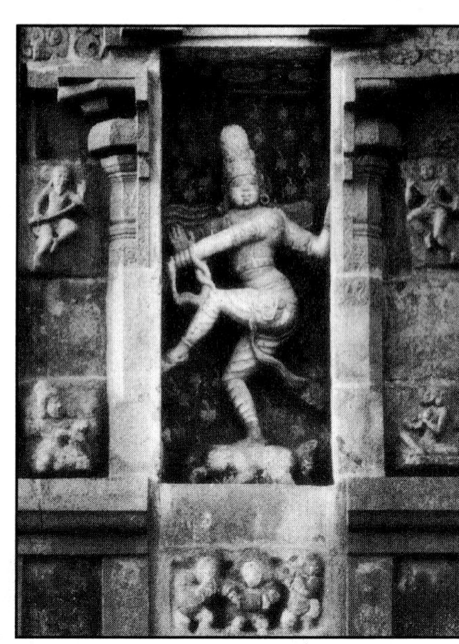

Naṭarāja

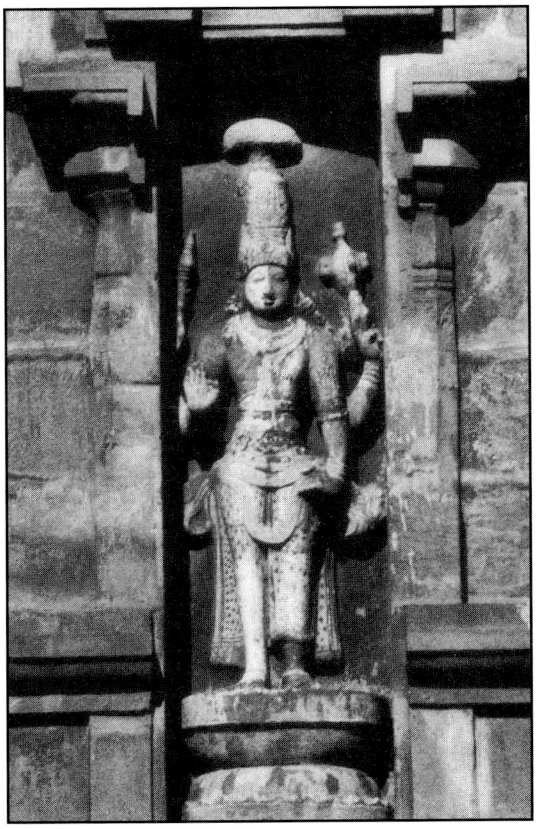

Harihara

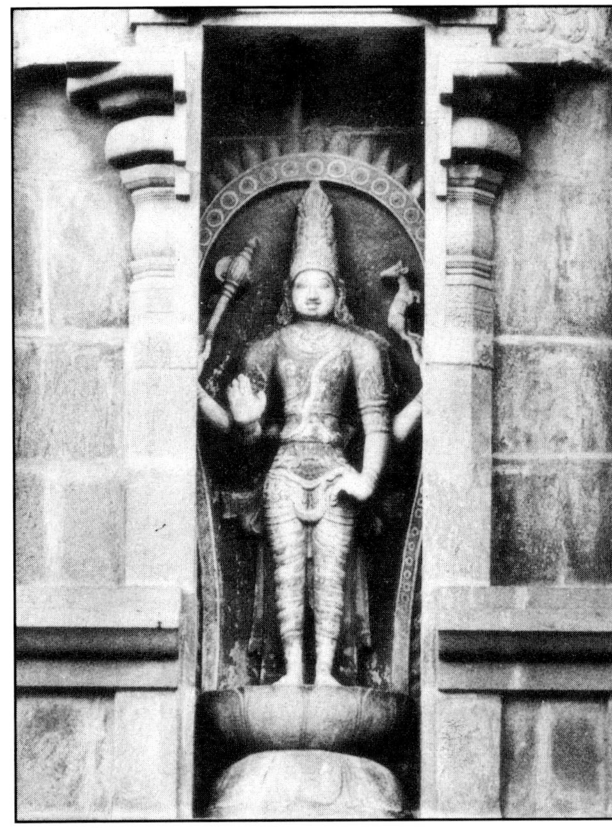

Candraśekhara

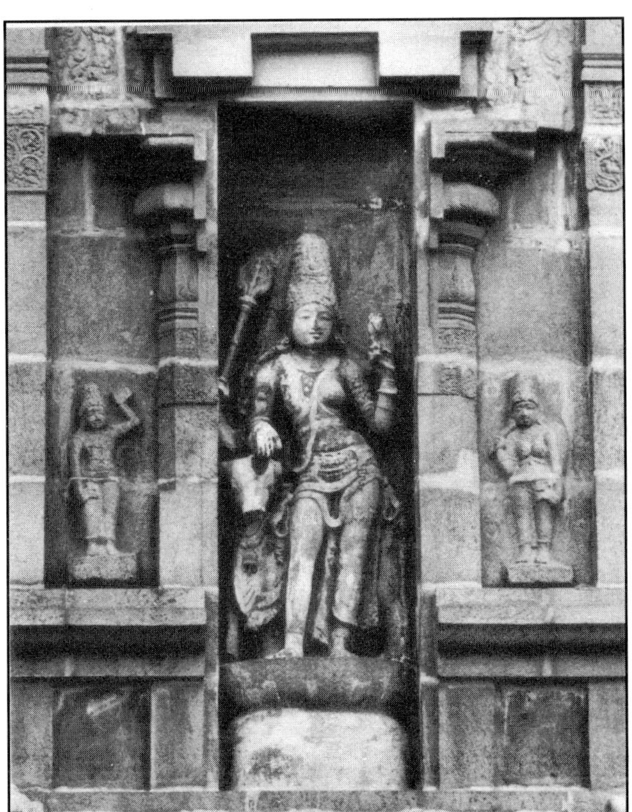

Ardhanārīśvara

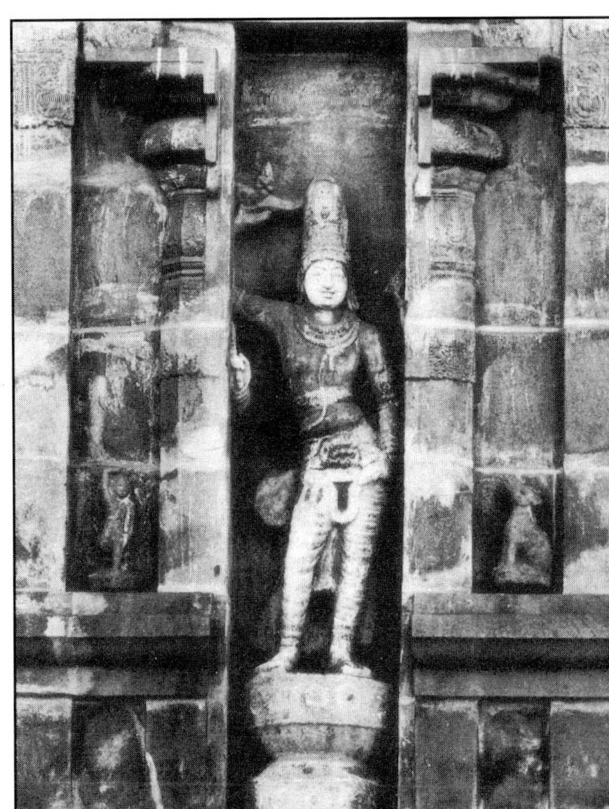

Gaṅgadhara

Plate 3. Sanctuary-tower, iconography of the ground floor

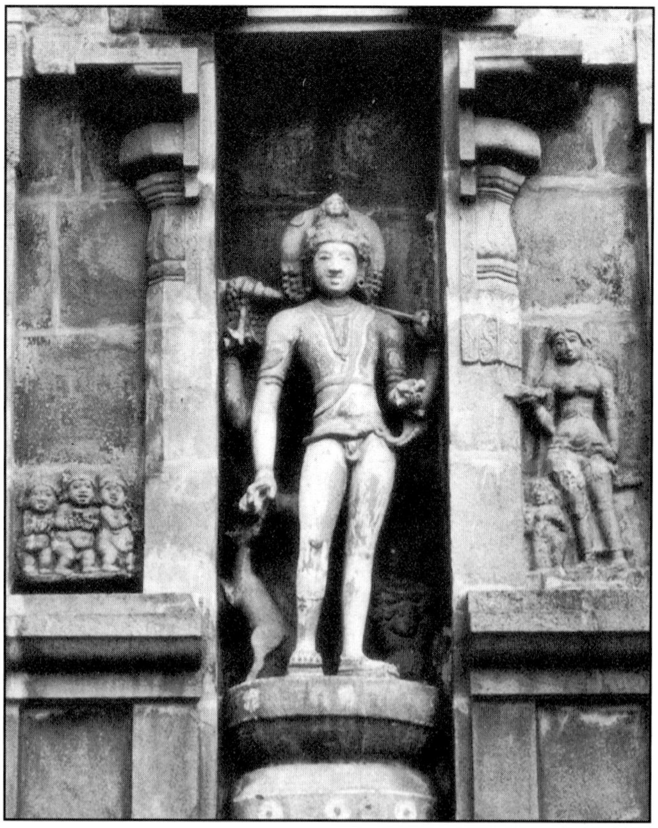

Bikṣāṭana

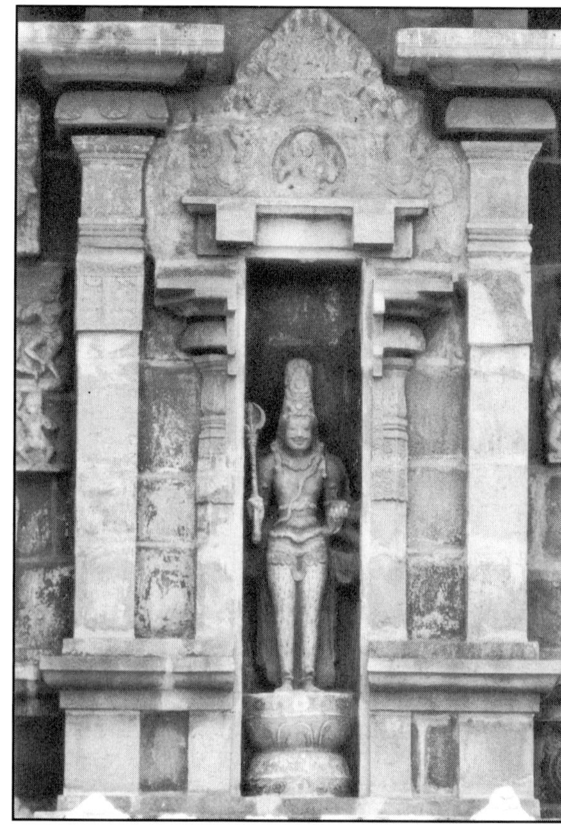

Vīrabhadra

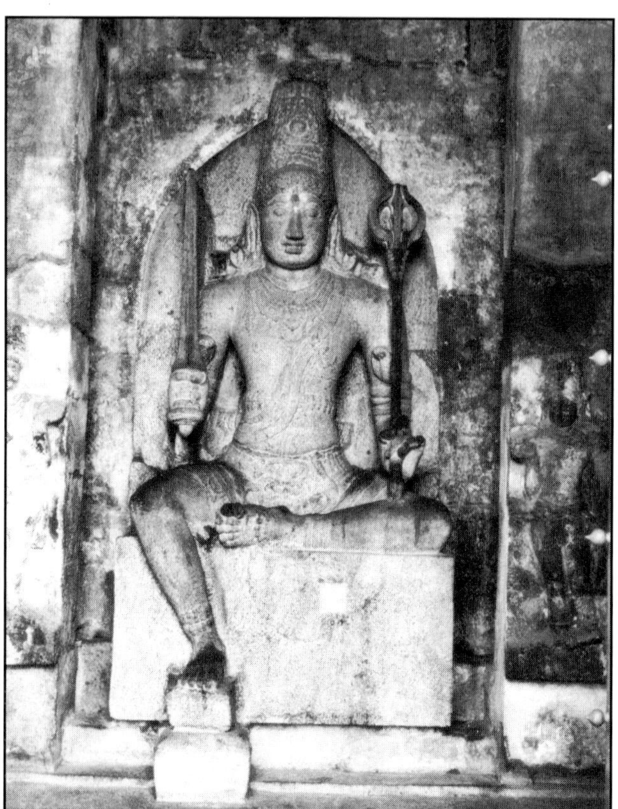

Rudra-Aghora

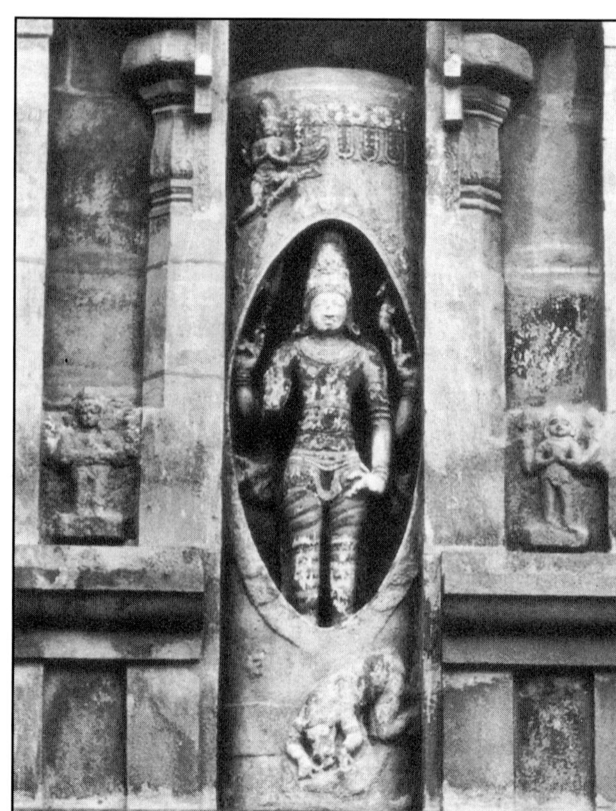

Liṅgodbhavamūrti

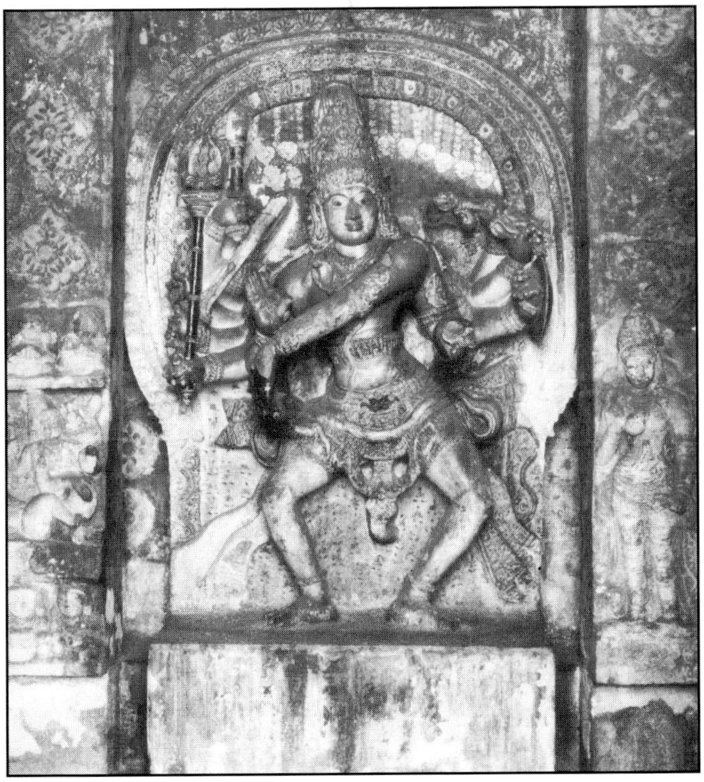

Dancing Śiva-Sadyojāta

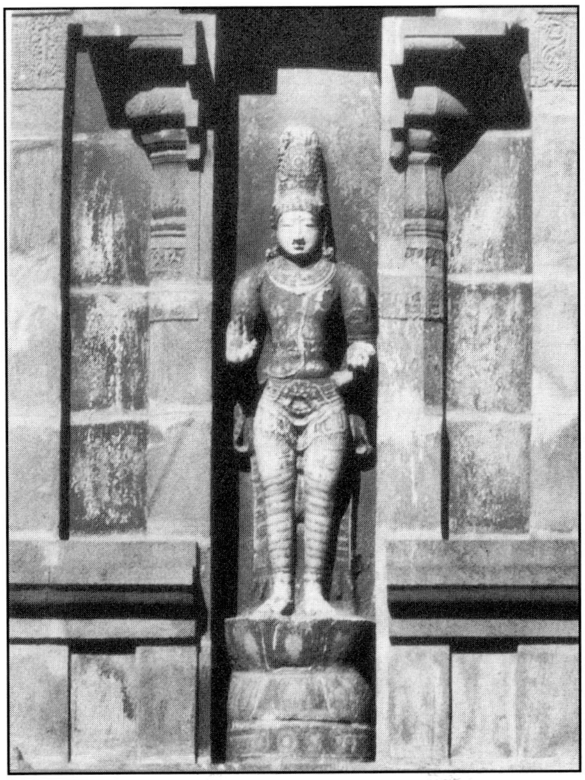

Candraśekhara

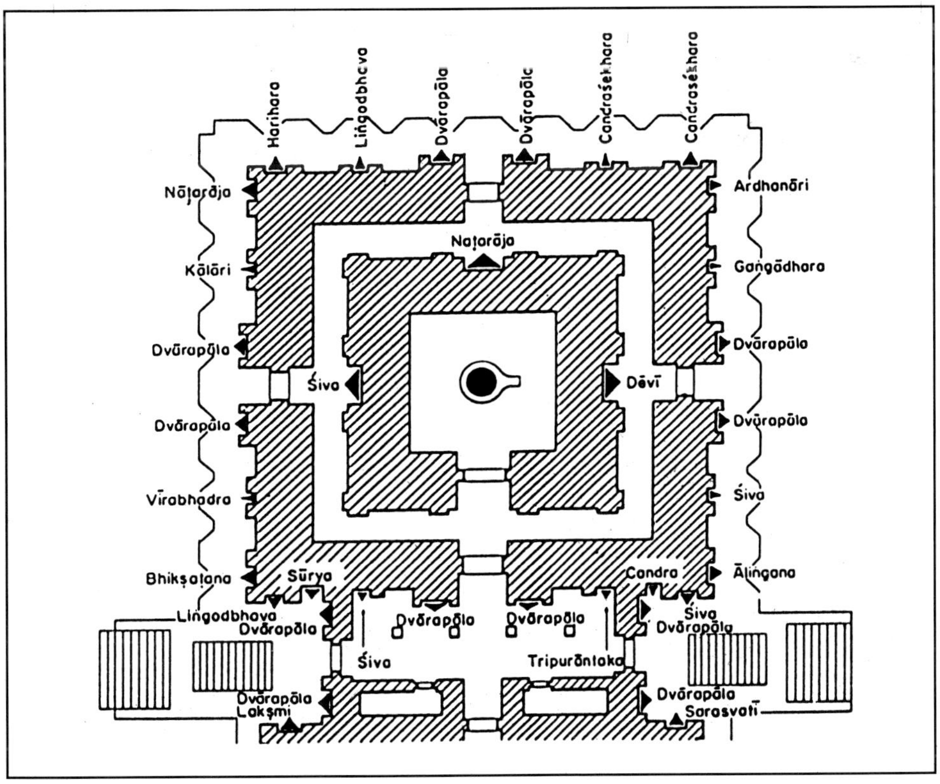

Iconography of the ground-floor of the sanctuary-tower

Plate 4. Sanctuary-tower, iconography of the ground floor

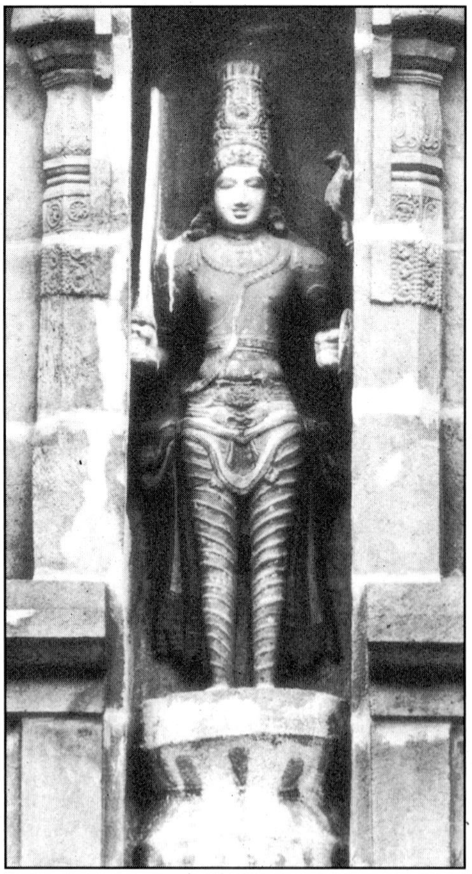

Śiva

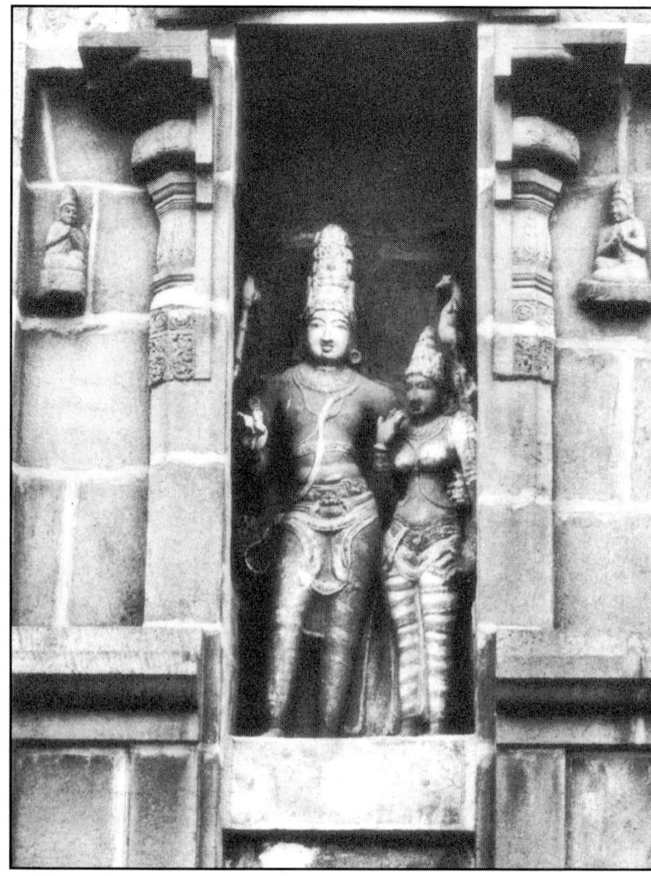

Āliṅgana

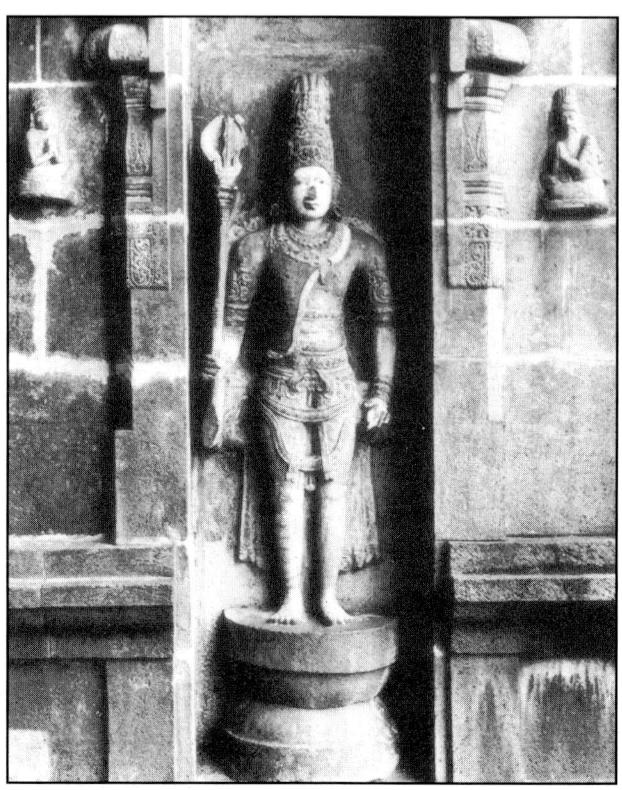

Śiva

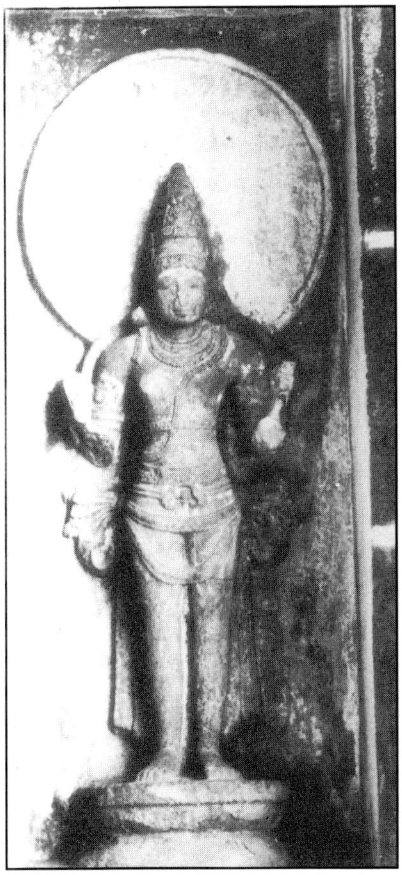

Candra

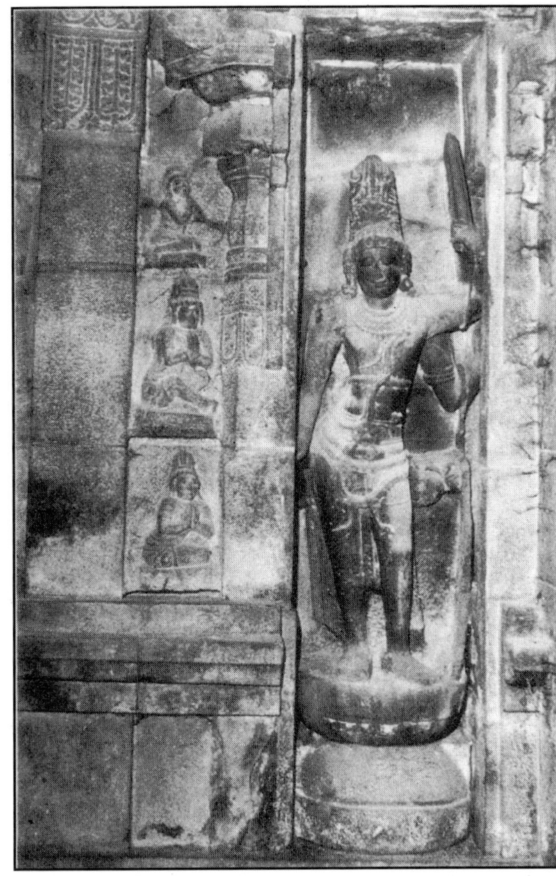

Tripurāntaka

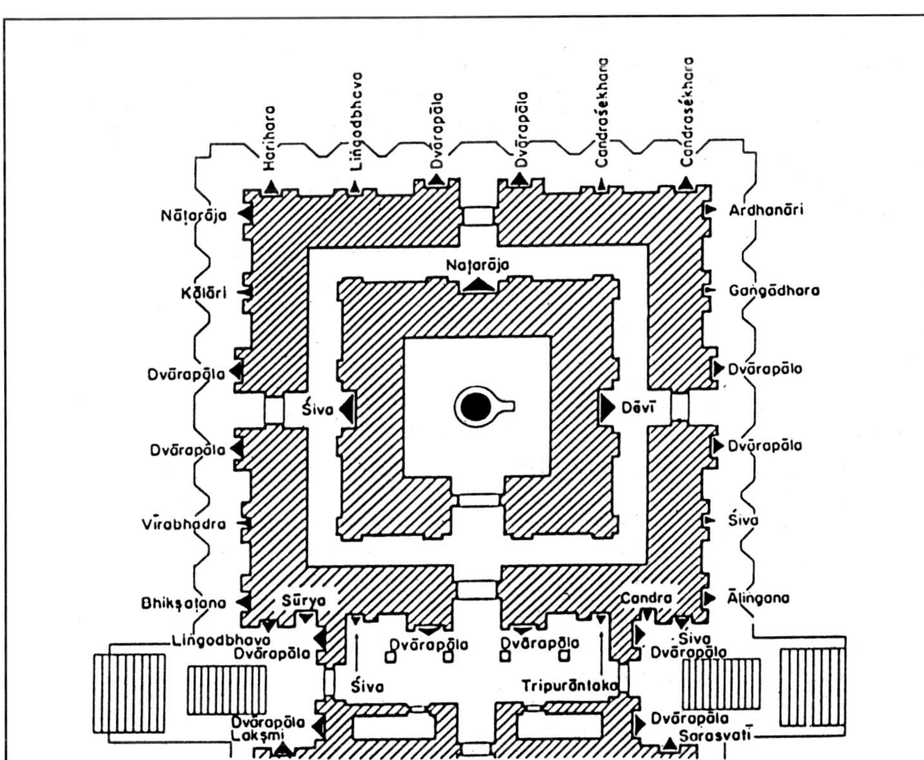

Iconography of the ground-floor of the sanctuary-tower

Plate 5. Sanctuary-tower, iconography of the upper floor

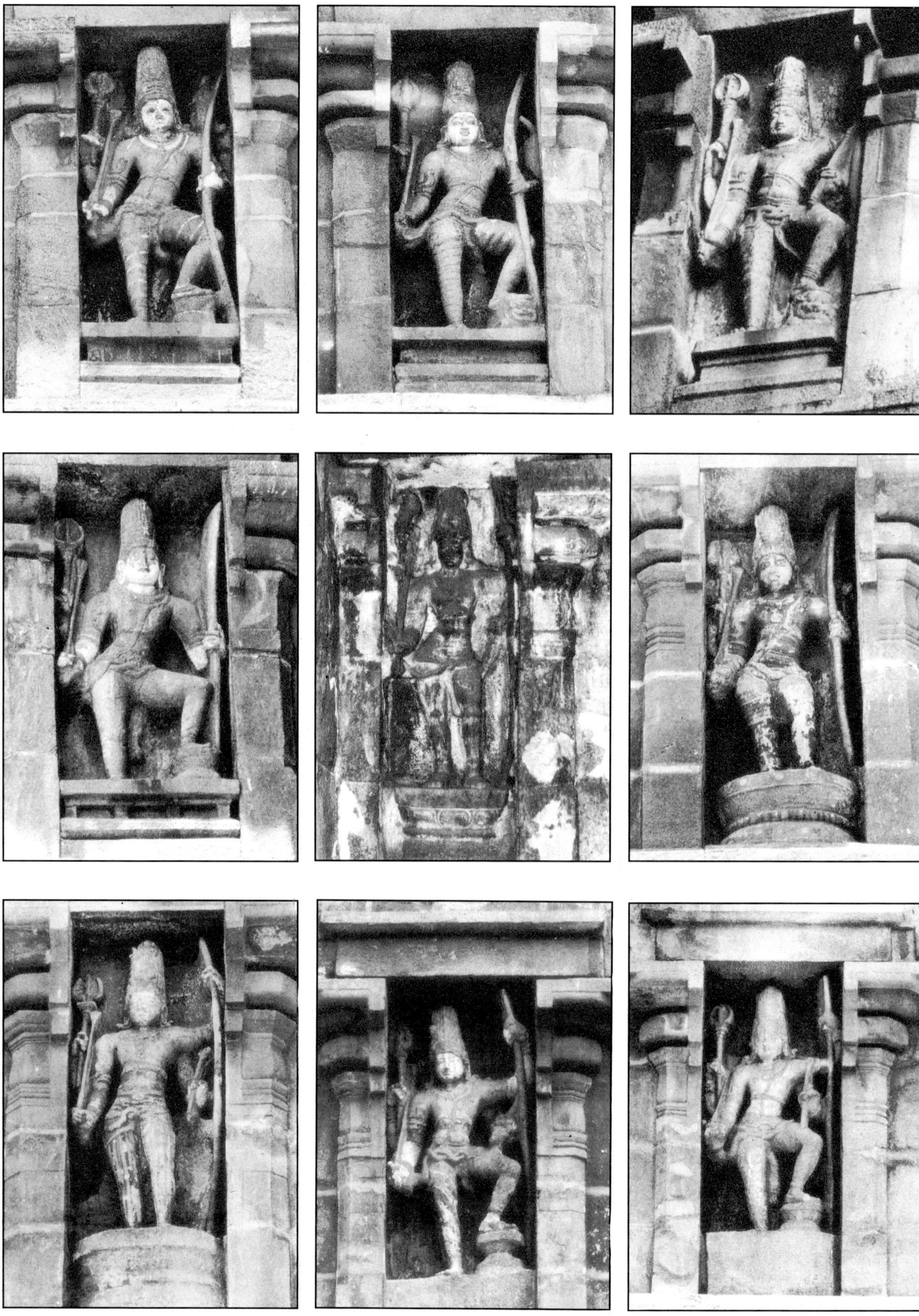

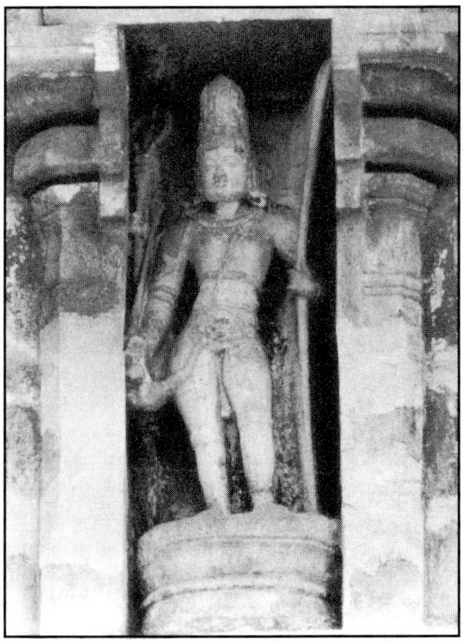

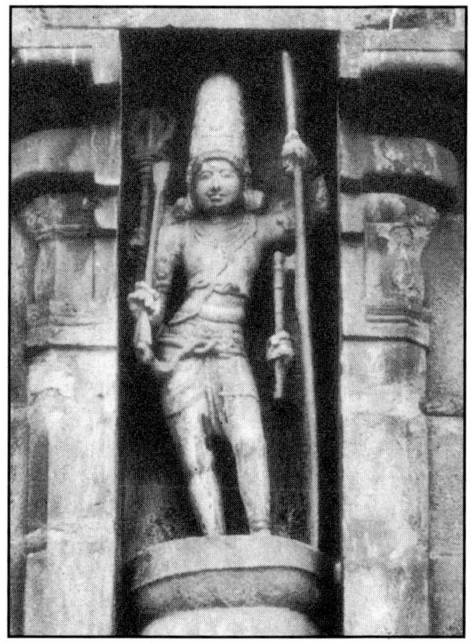

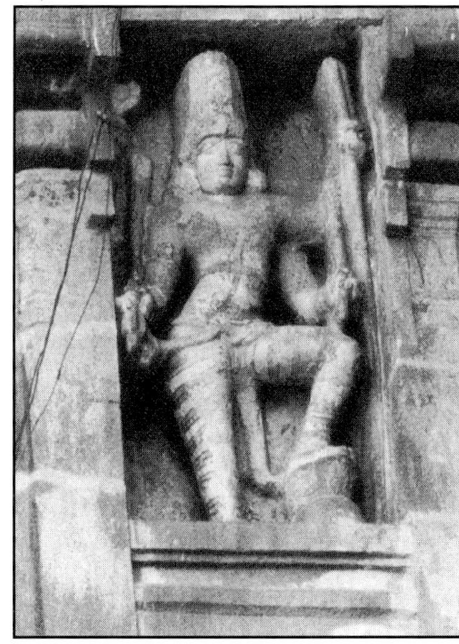

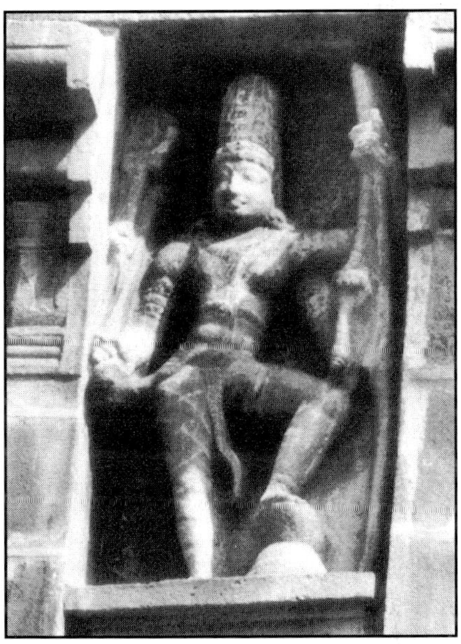

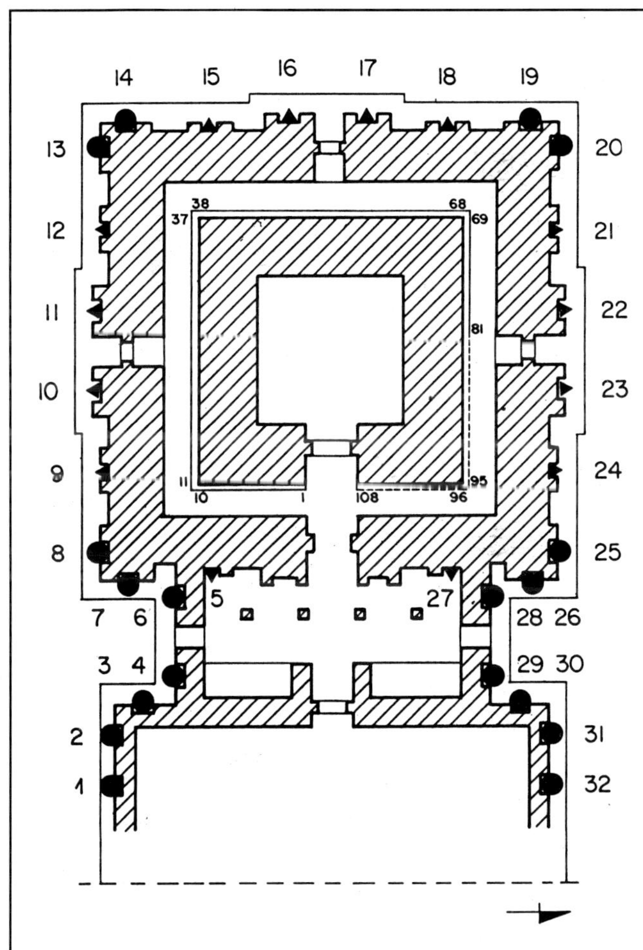

The thirty-two Tripurāntaka of the upper storey of the sanctuary-tower
●: corner figures with one leg on a pedestal
◀ : figures standing on both legs
(1-108: panels of the corridor with dance poses)

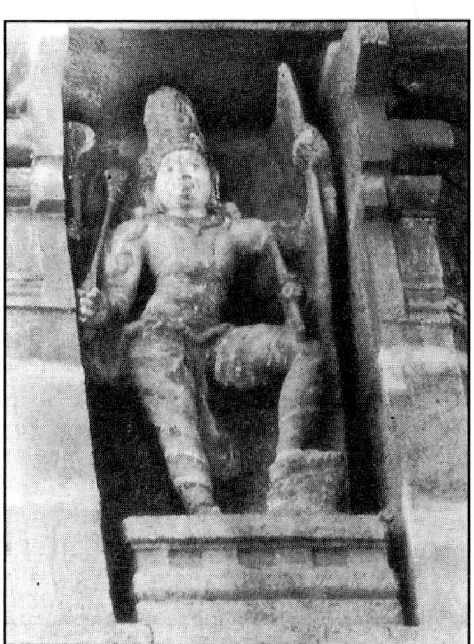

Plate 6. Sanctuary-tower, iconography of the upper floor

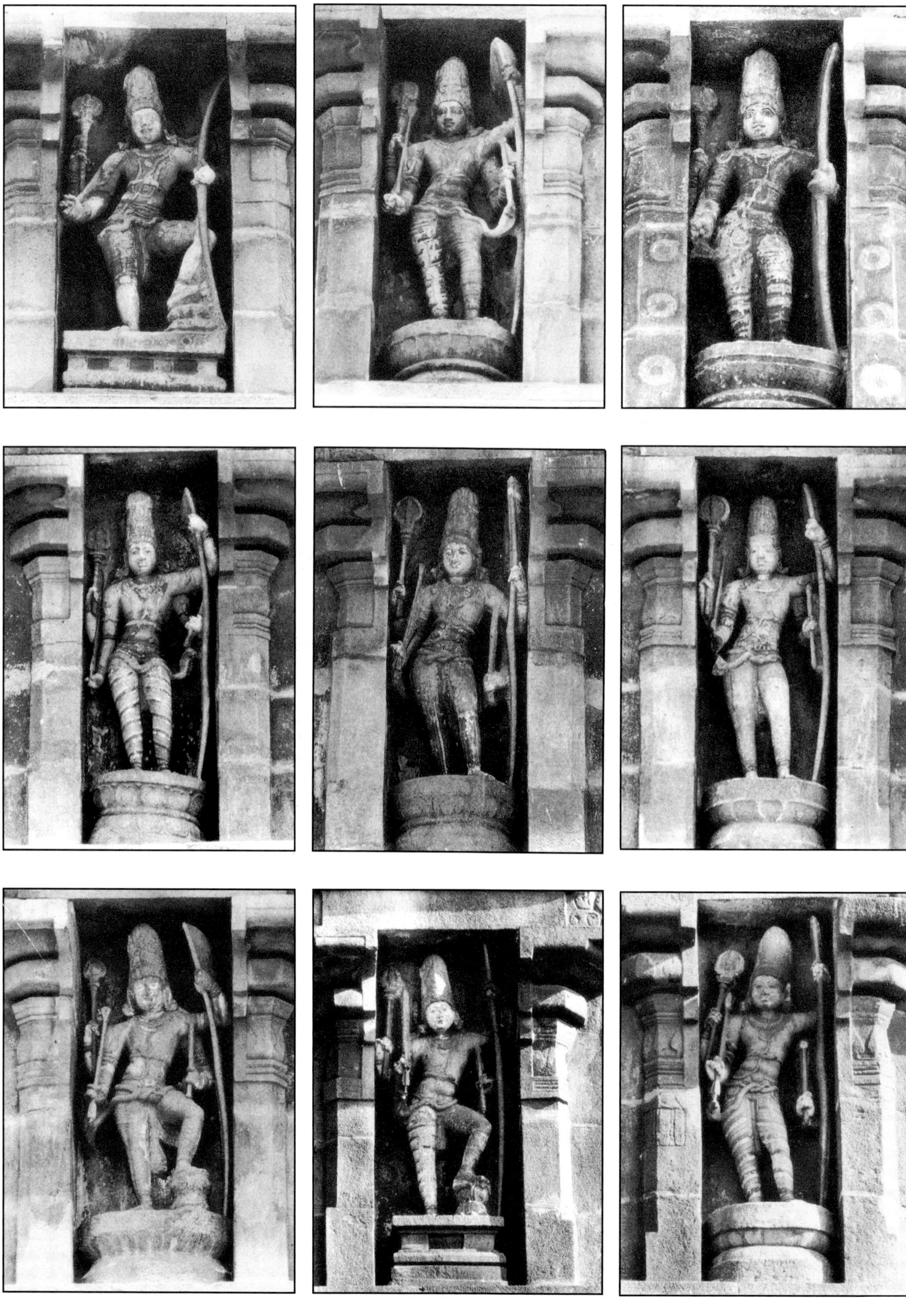

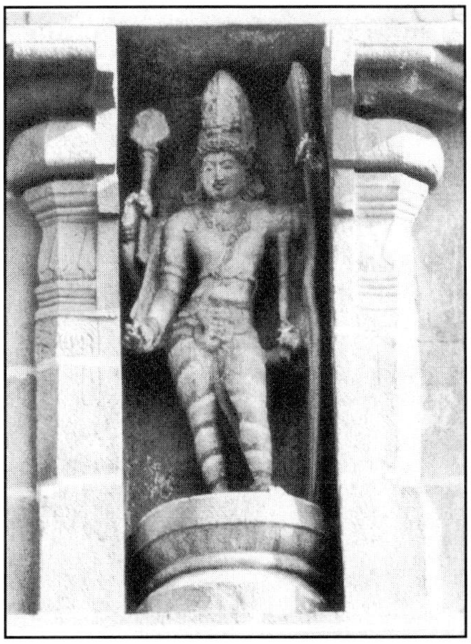
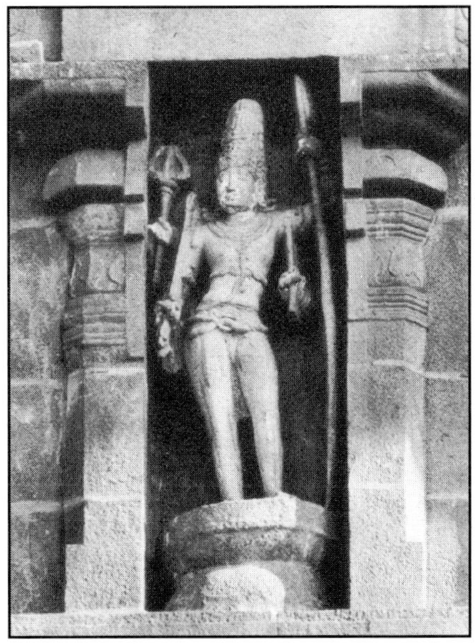
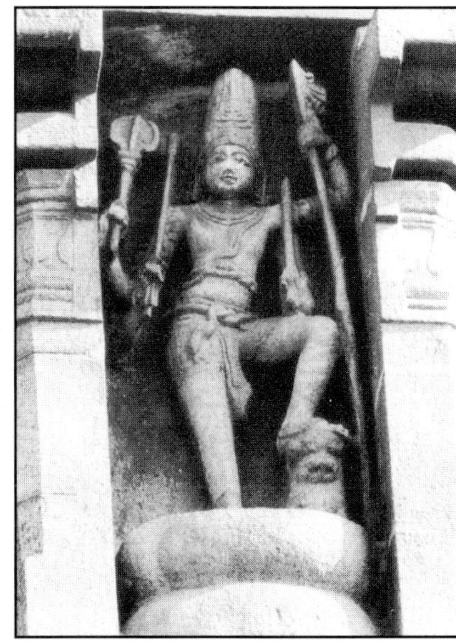
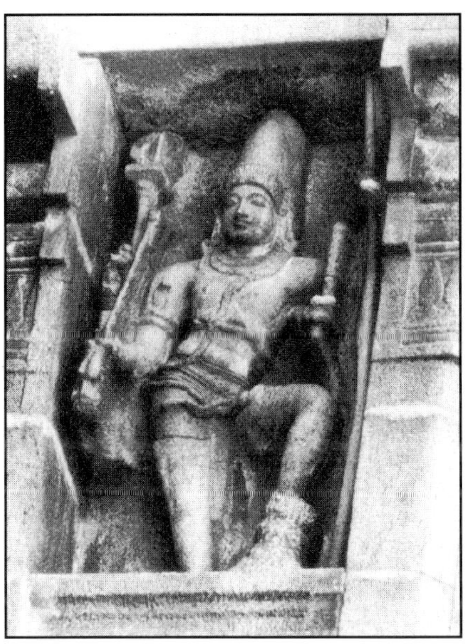
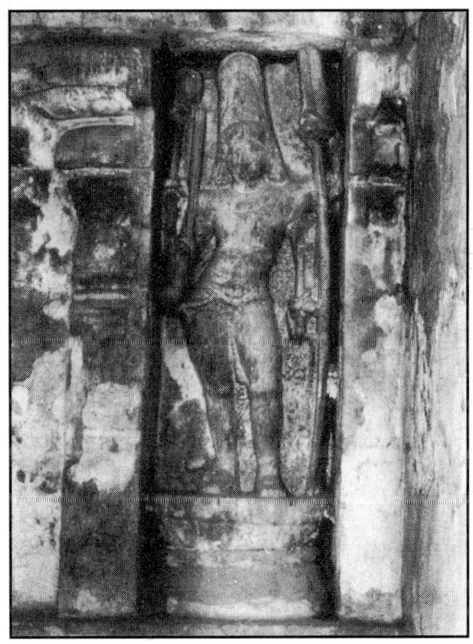
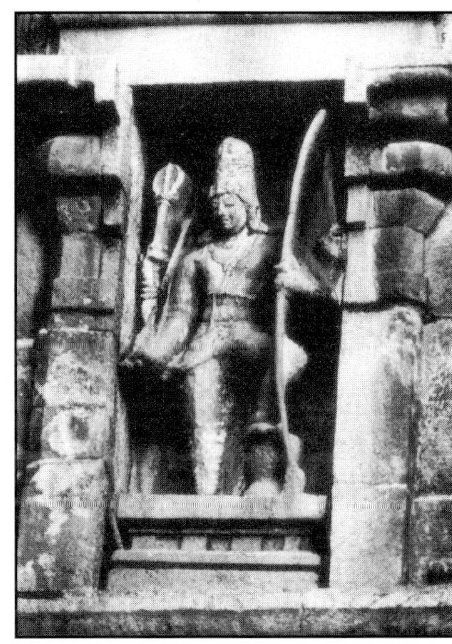
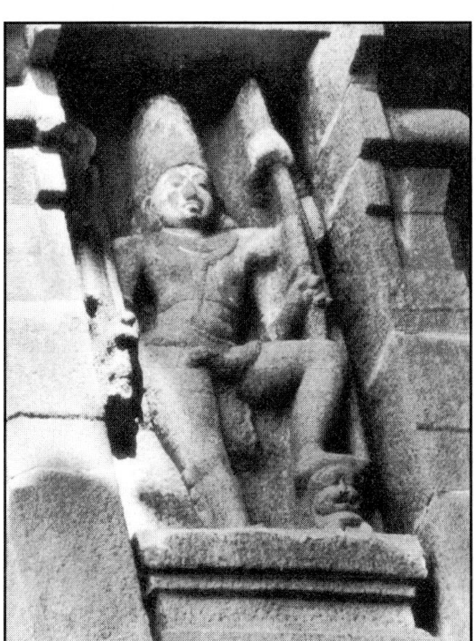
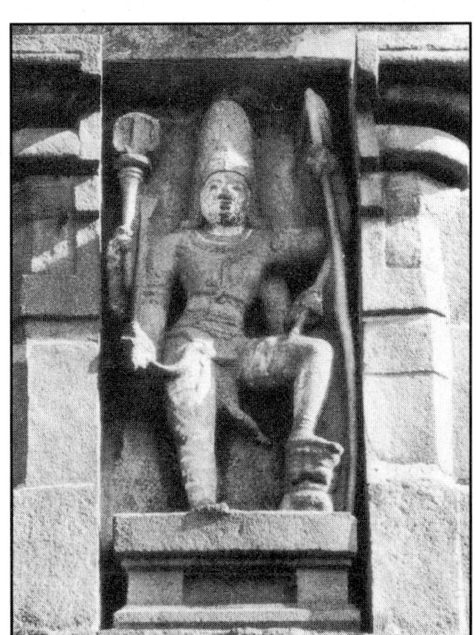
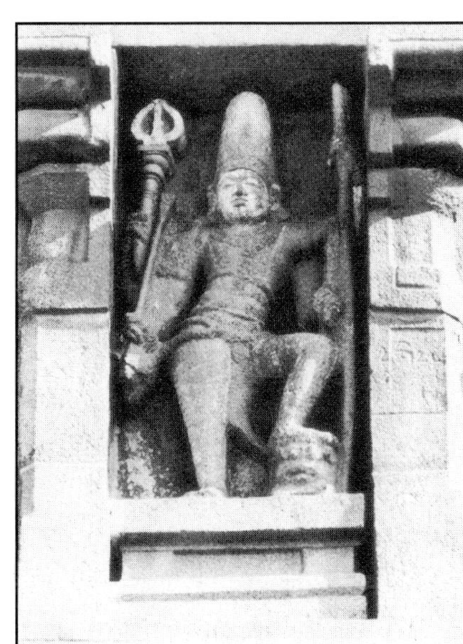

Plate 7. Pillared hall, iconography

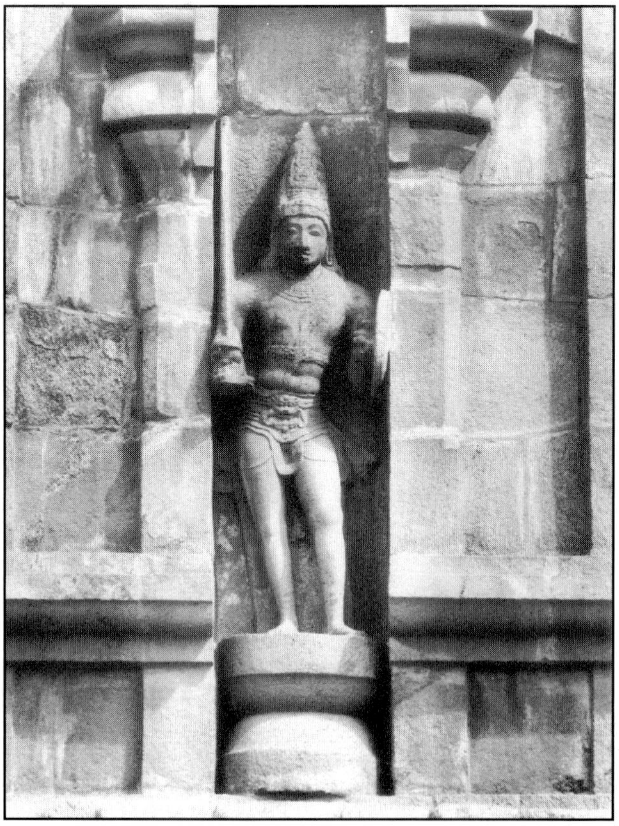

Warrior (4)

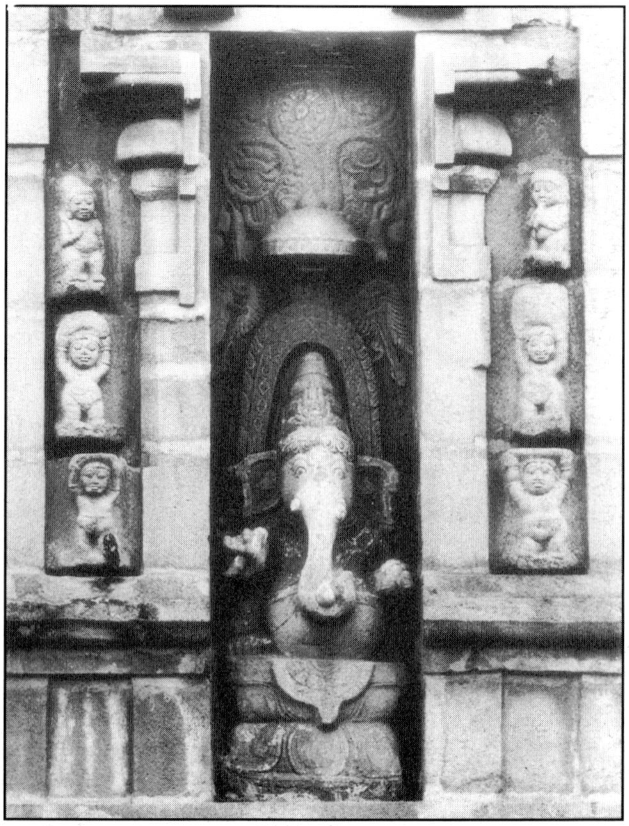

Gaṇapati

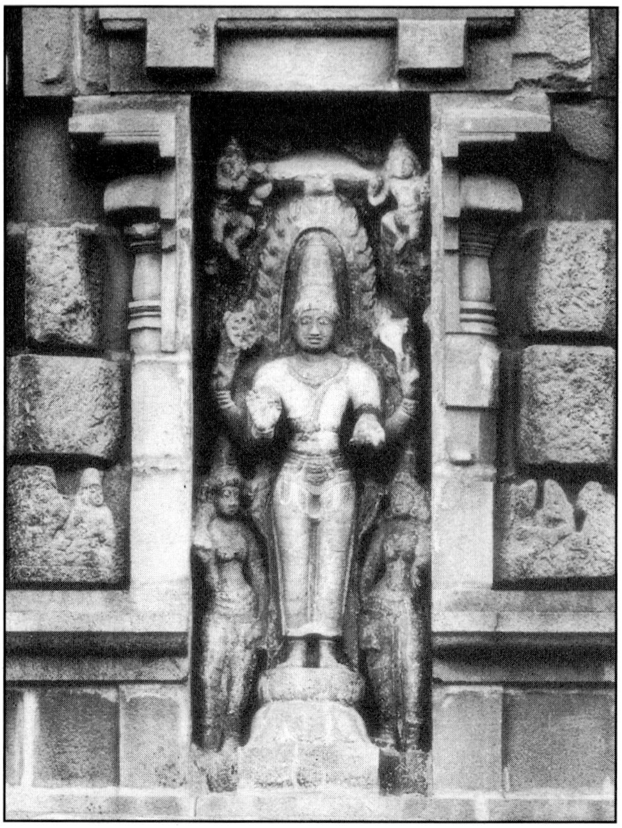

Viṣṇu

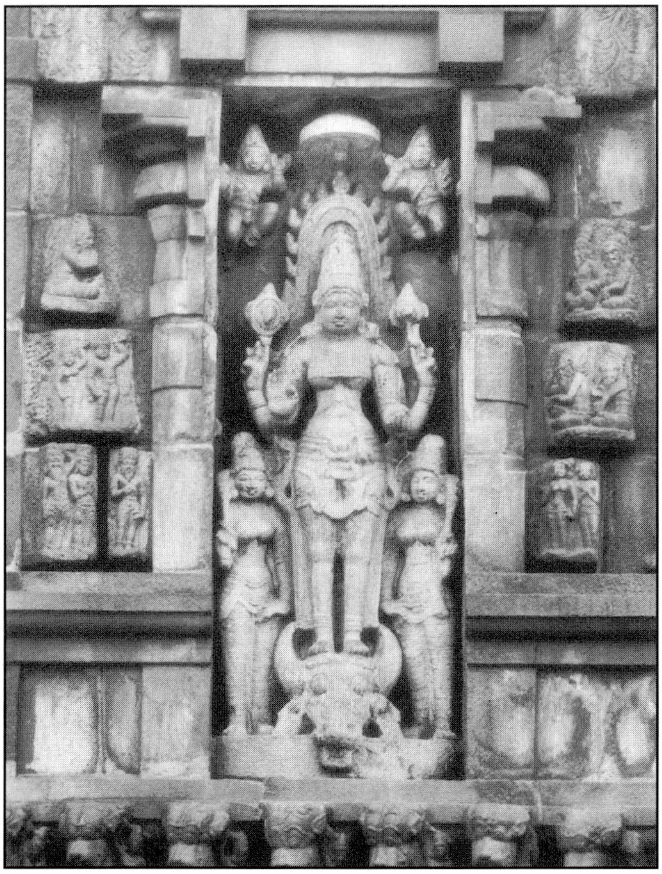

Durgā

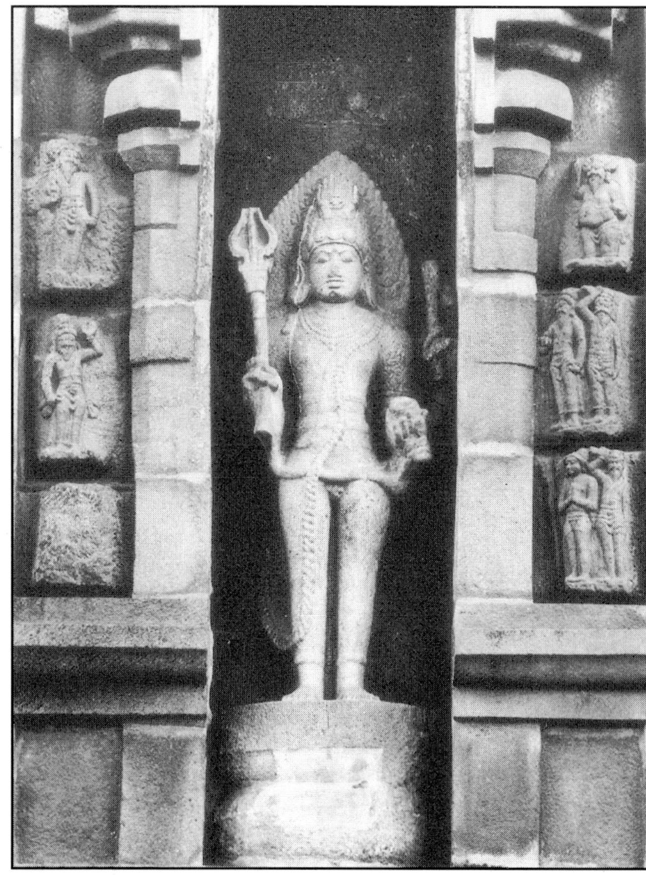

Bhairava

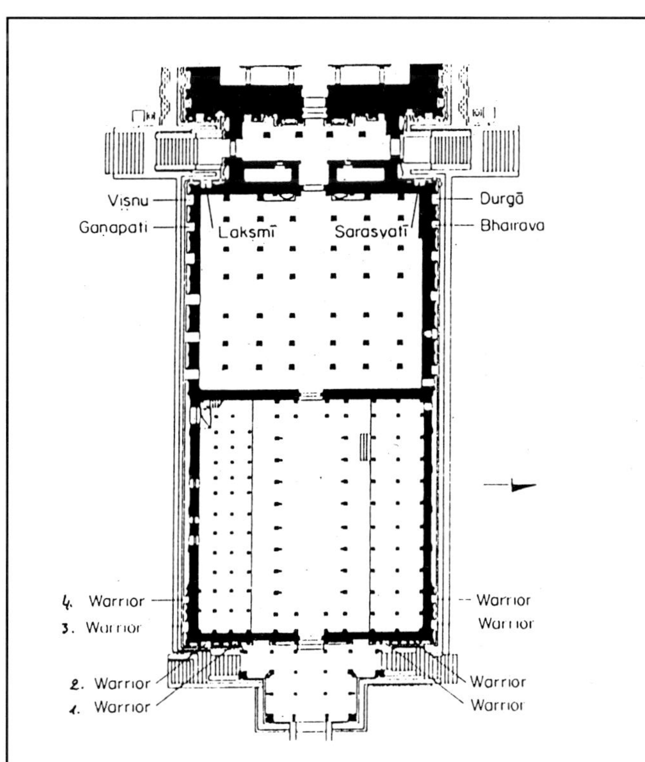

The figures of the pillared hall

Plate 8. Pillared hall, iconography

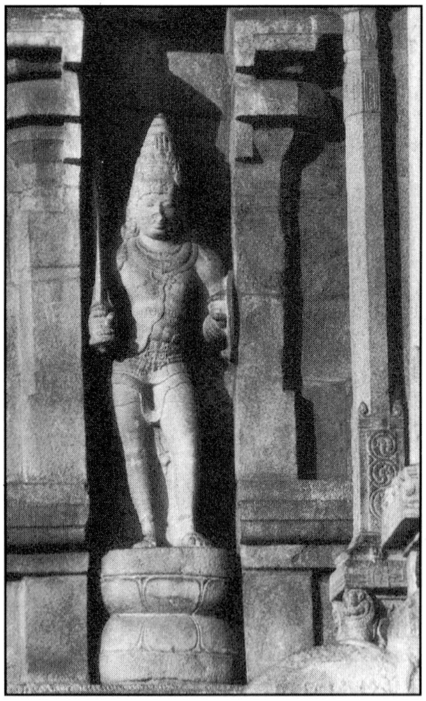

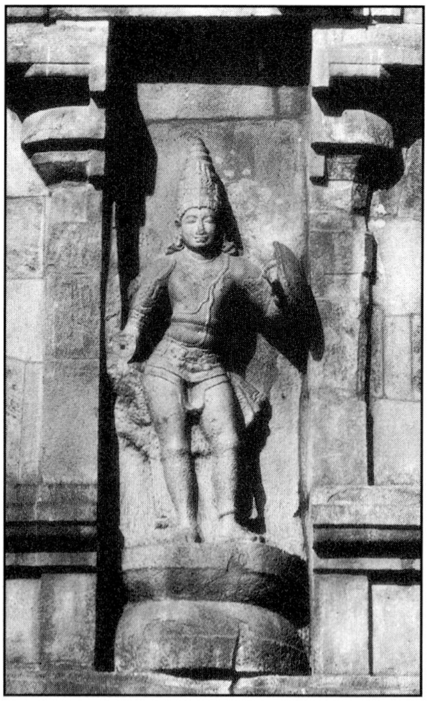

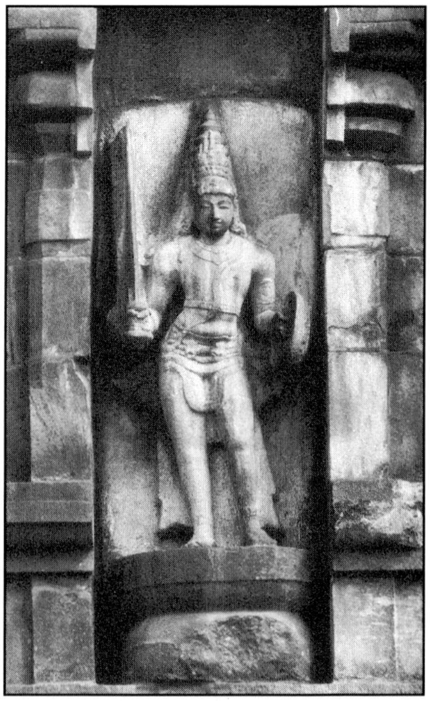

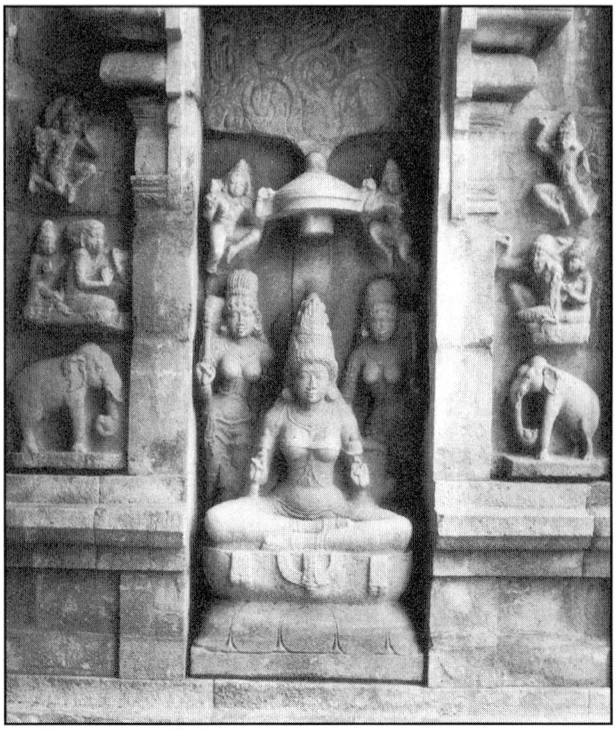

Lakṣmī

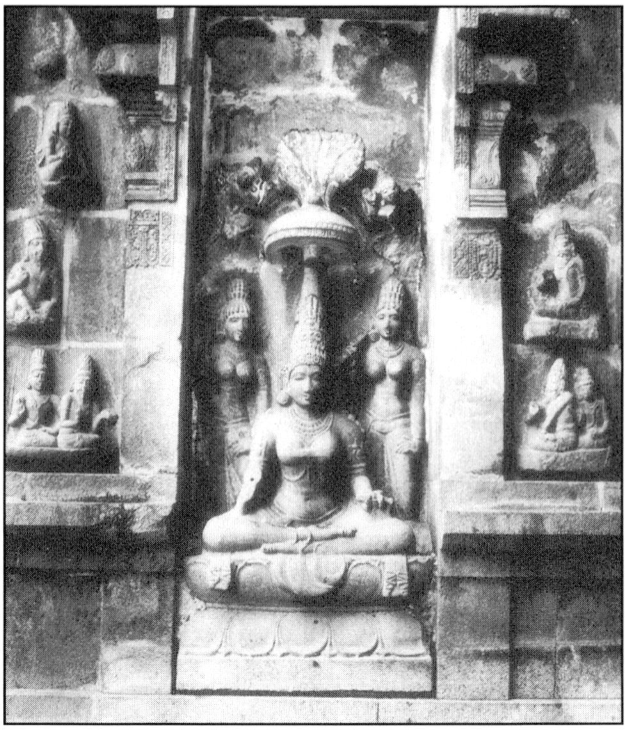

Sarasvatī

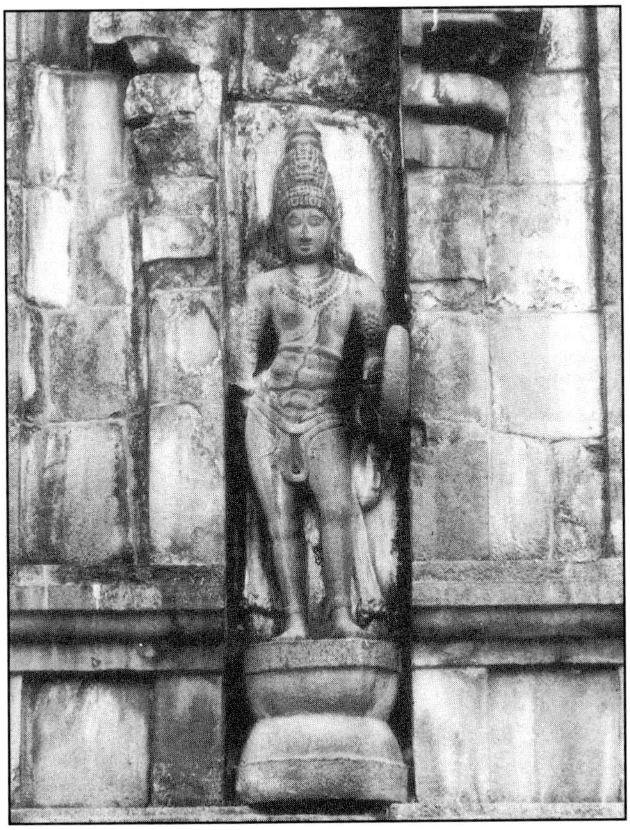
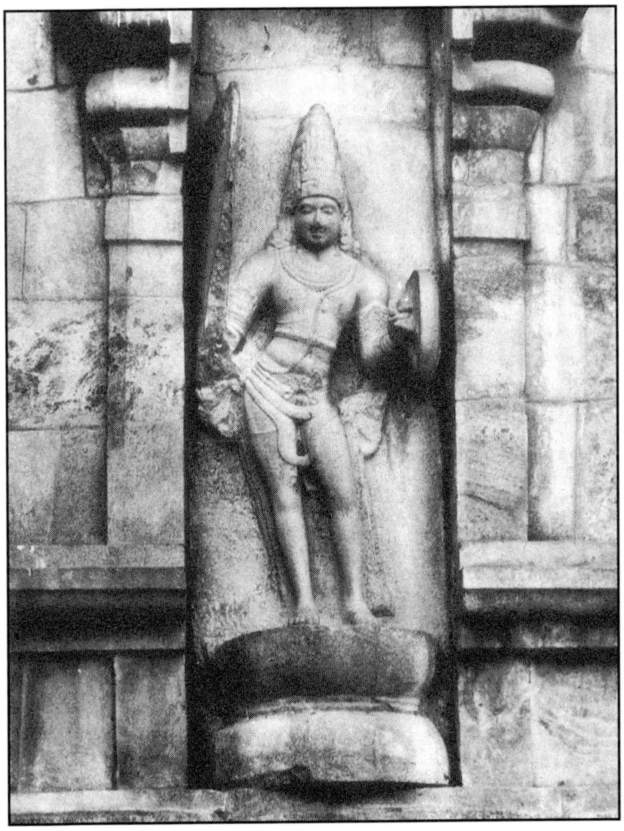
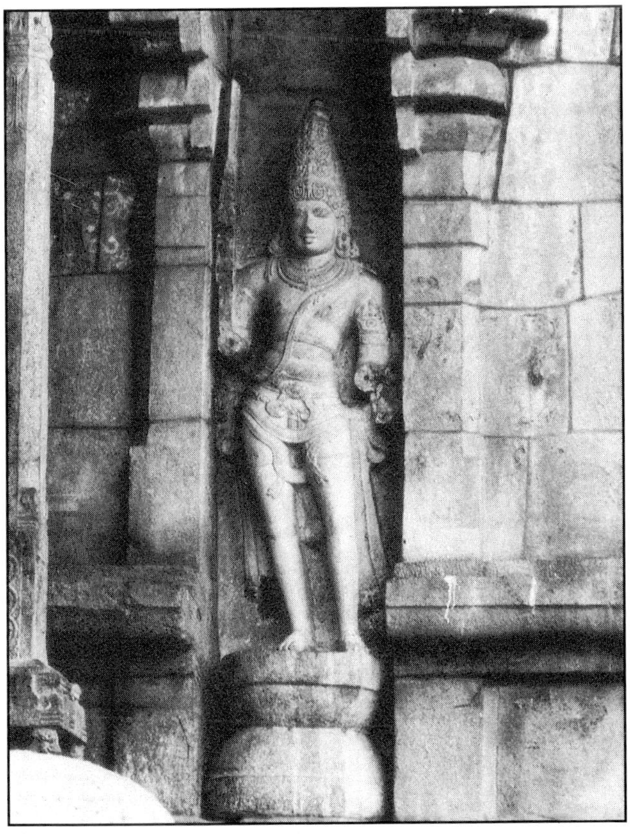
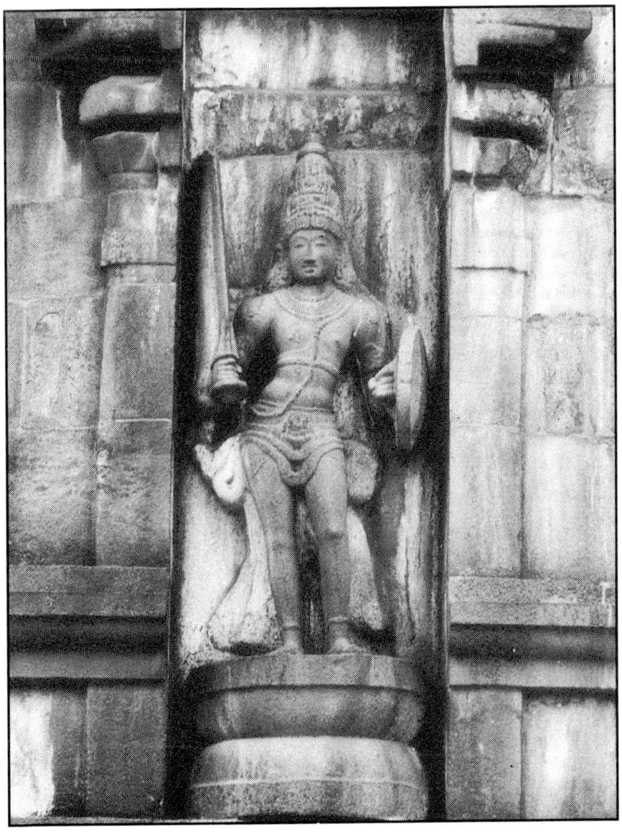

Plate 9. Southern stairway of the vestibule, East face

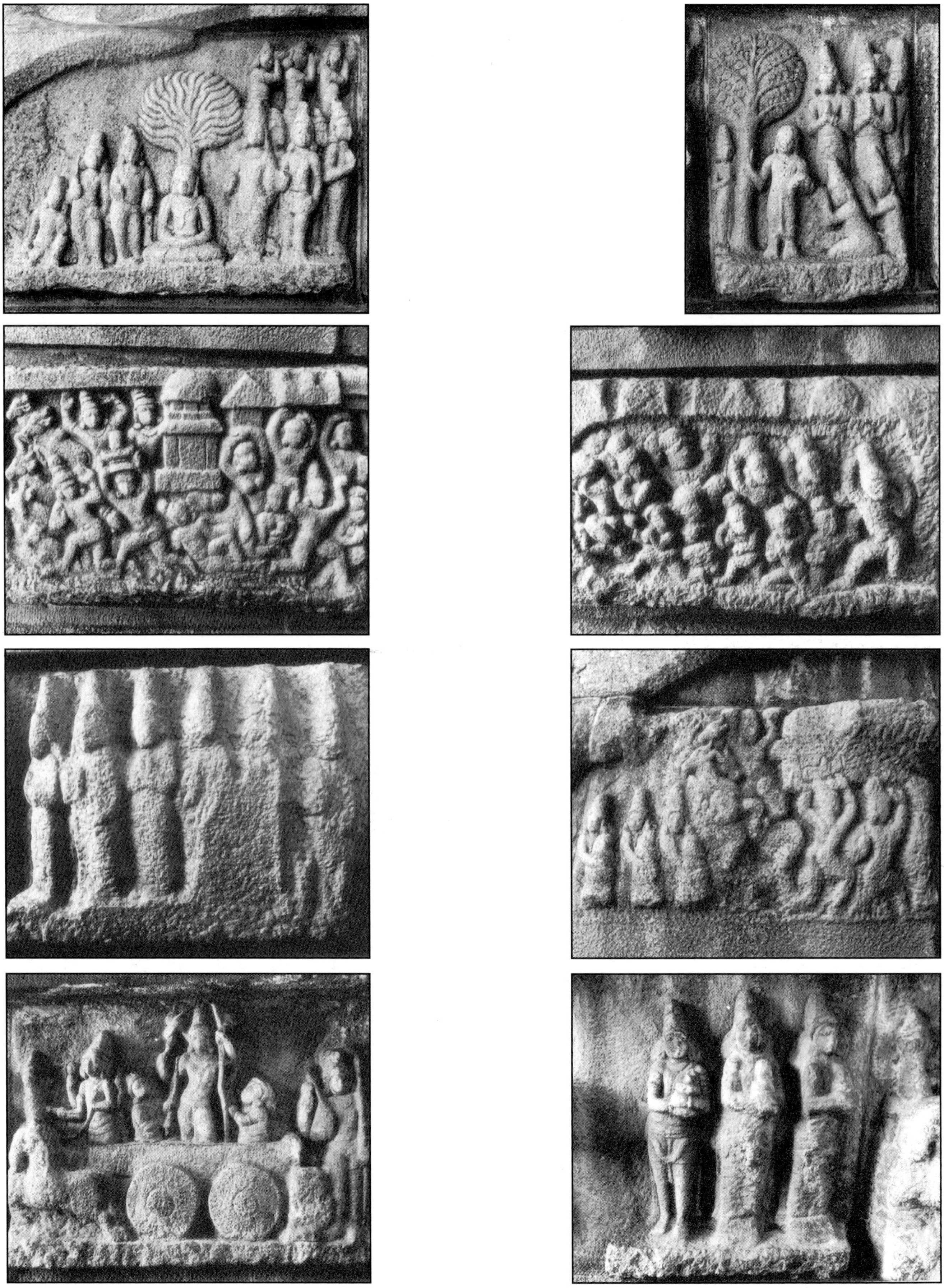

1 to 9 – Tripurāntaka's story

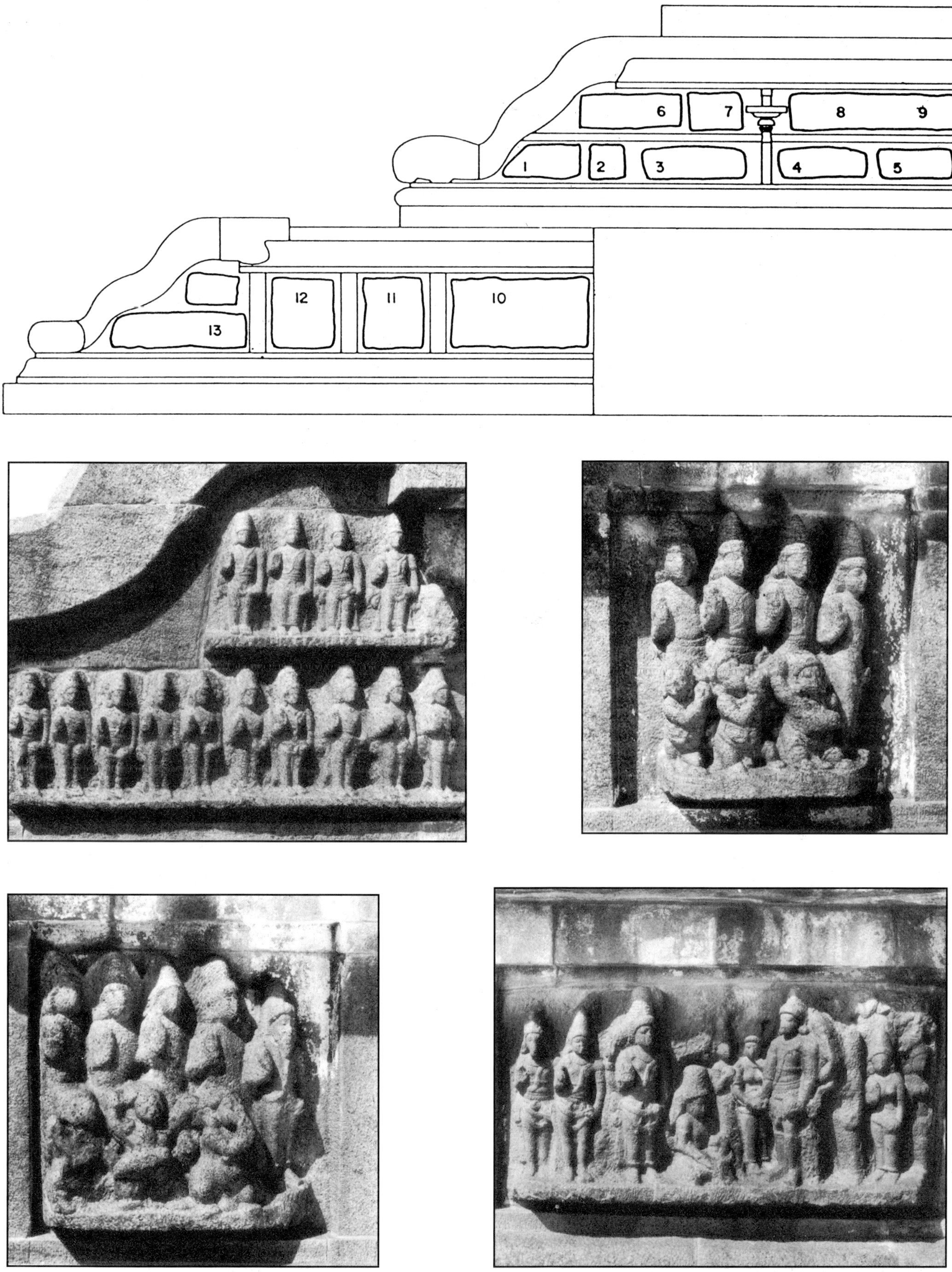

10 to 13 – Marriage of Śiva

Plate 10. Southern stairway of the vestibule, West face

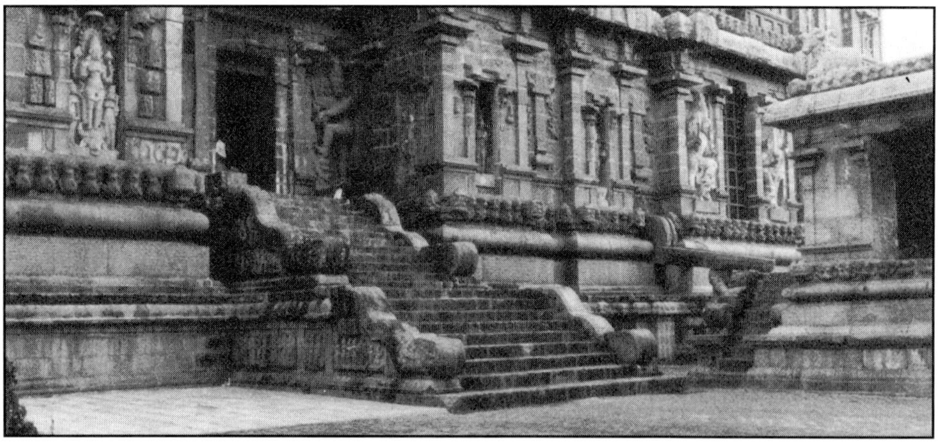

The northern stairway

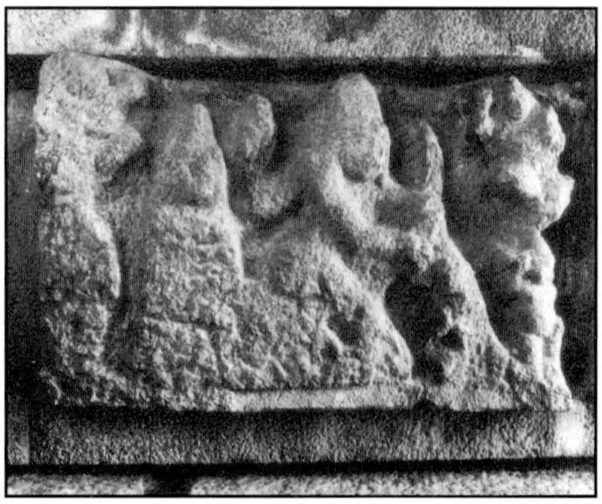

1 – Anugrahamūrti

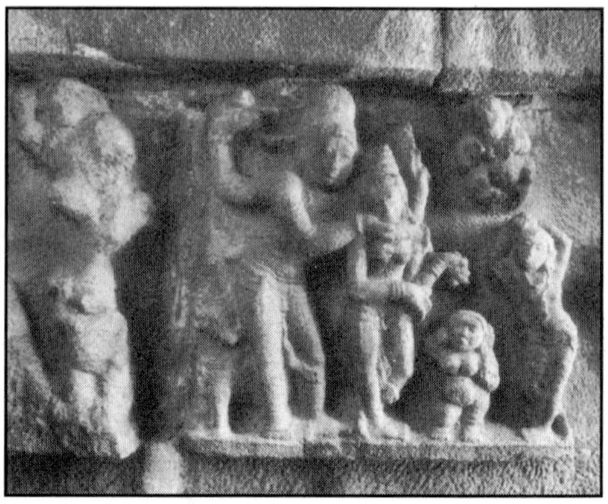

2 – Gaṅgādhara

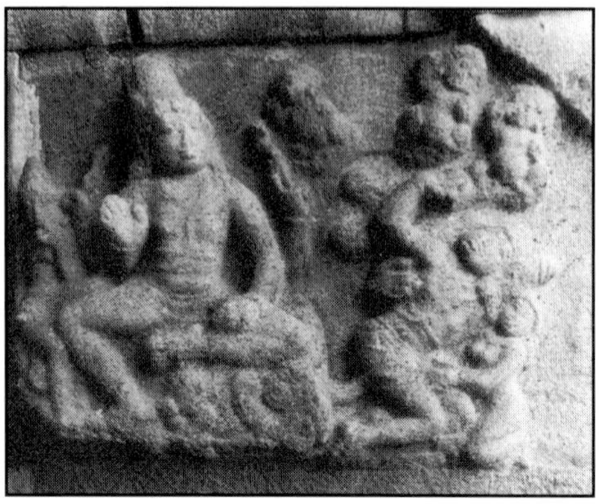

3 – Kamāntaka

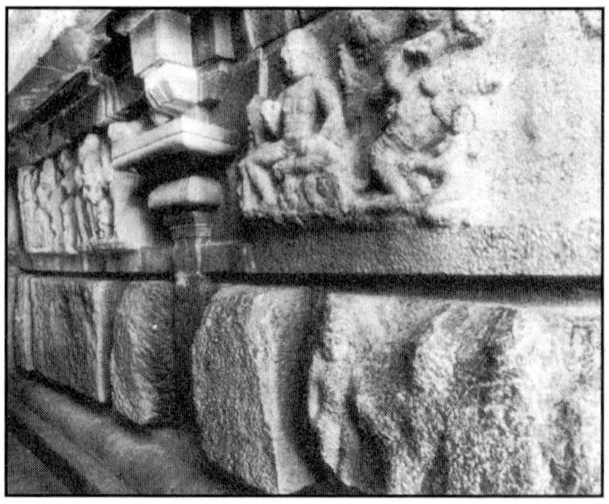

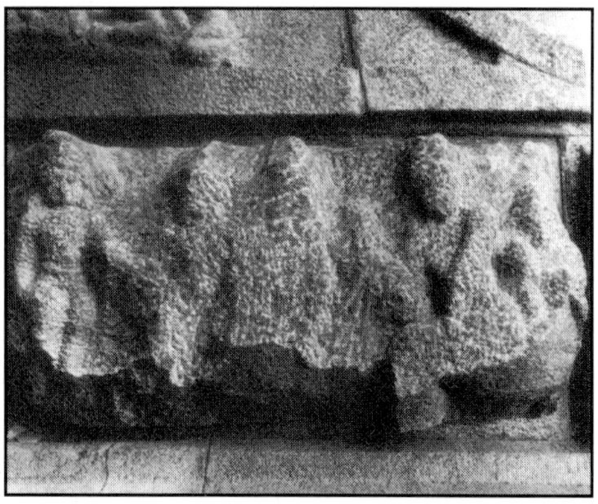

5 – Anugrahamūrti

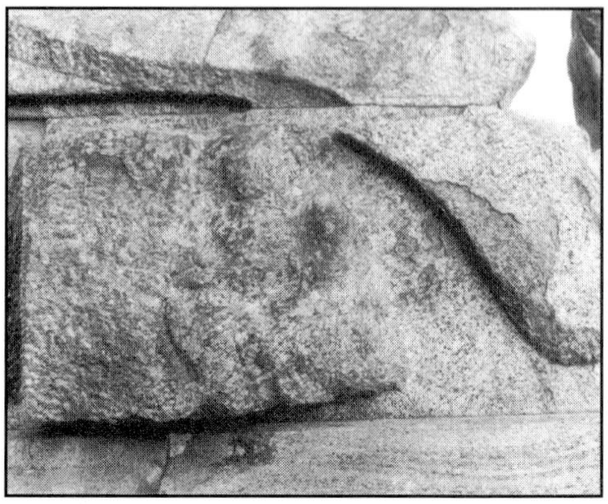

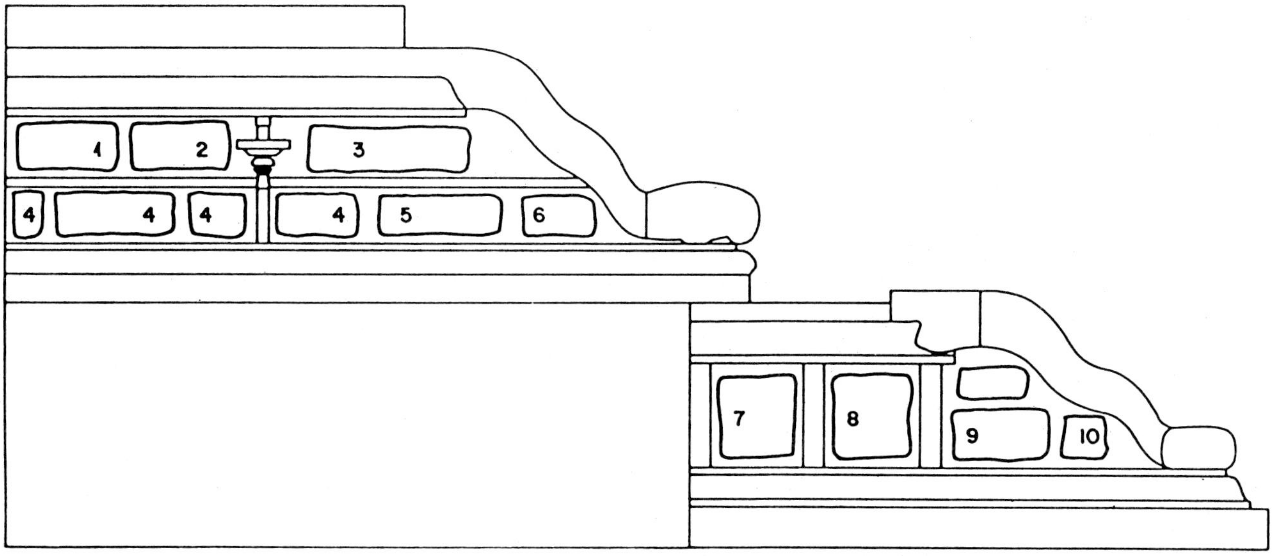

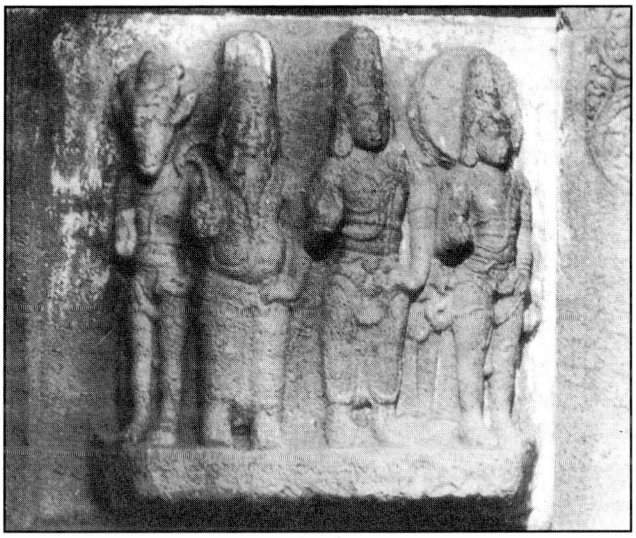

7 – Nandikeśvara, Nārada, Indra, Sūrya

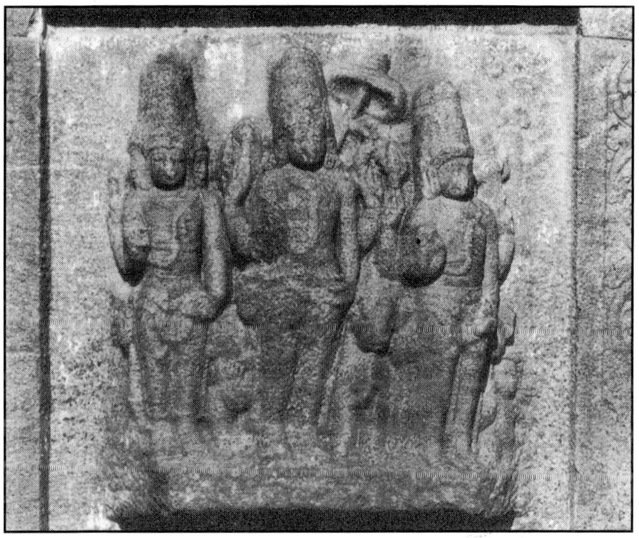

8 – Brahmā, Śiva, Viṣṇu

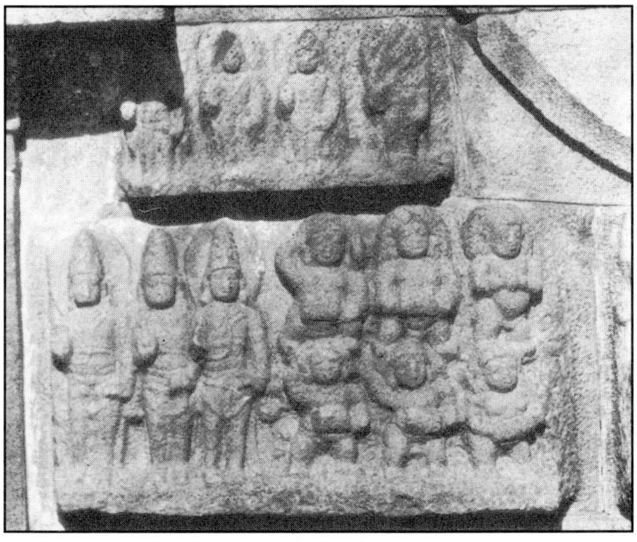

9 – The seven images

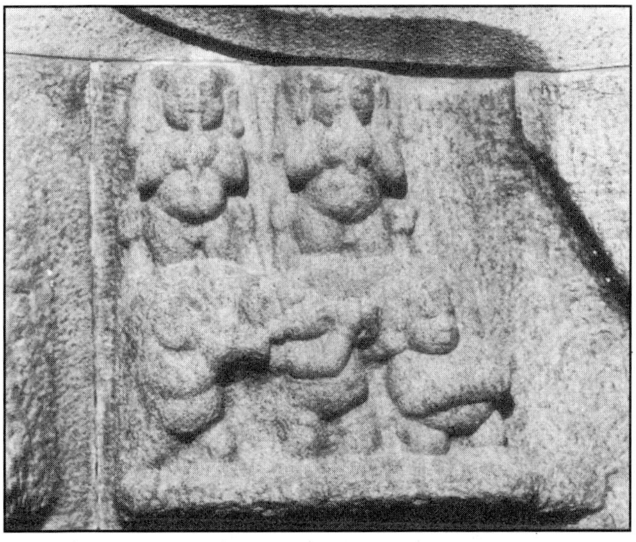

Plate 11. Northern stairway of the vestibule, West face

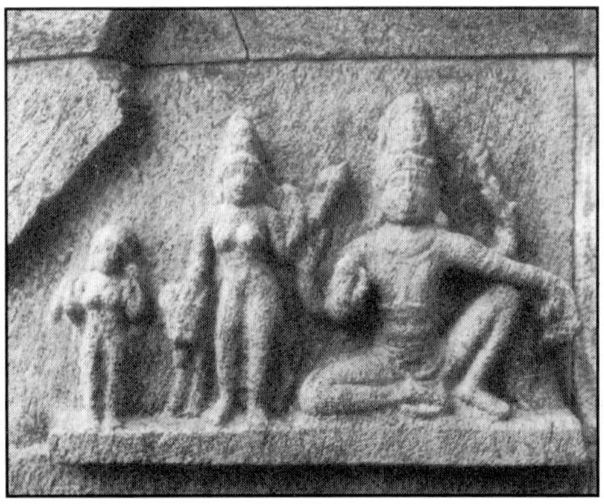

1 – Śiva and Pārvatī

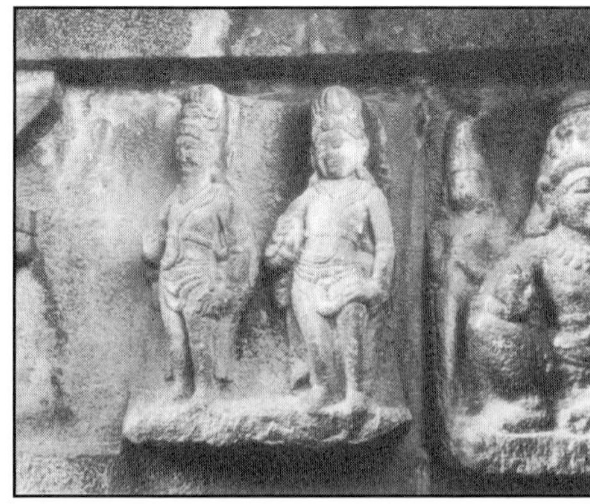

2 to 3 – Sages and gods

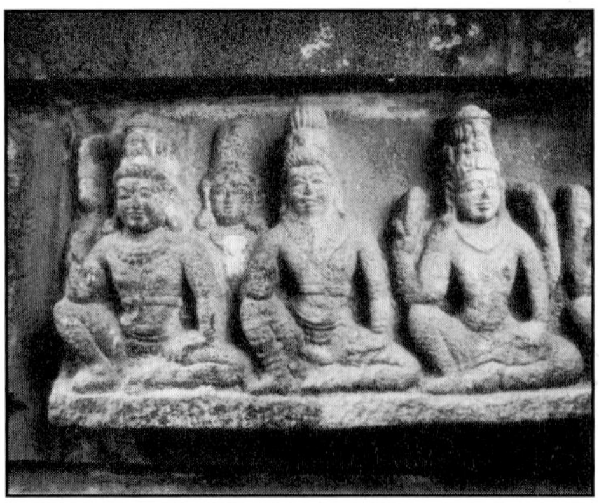

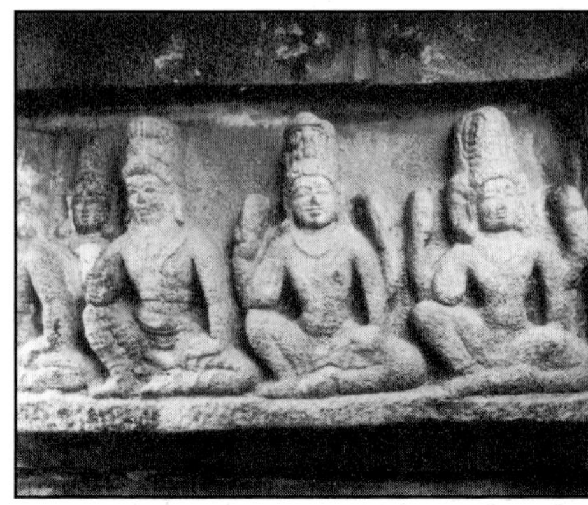

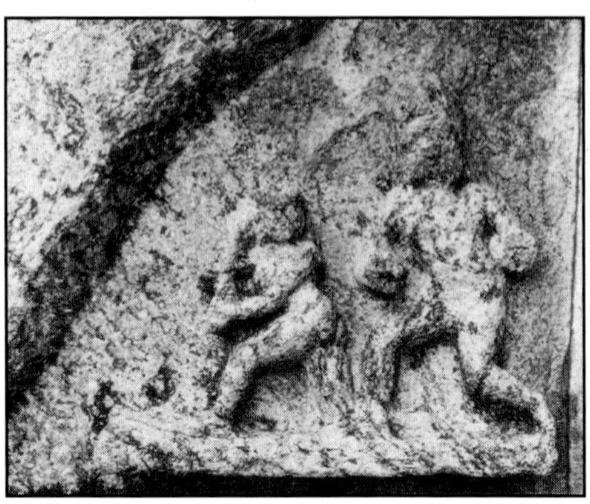

4 to 6 – Sacrifice of Dakṣa

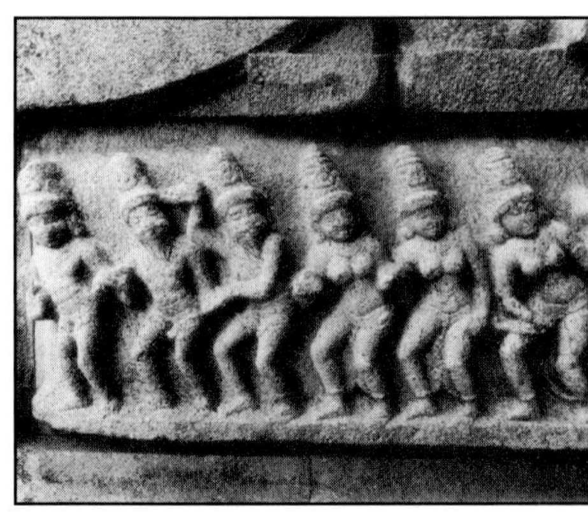

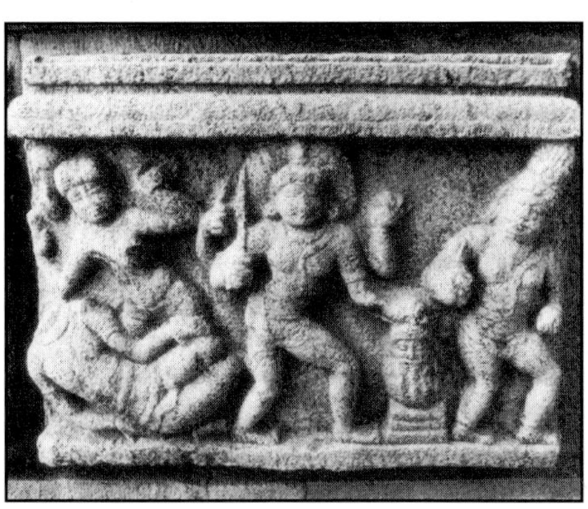

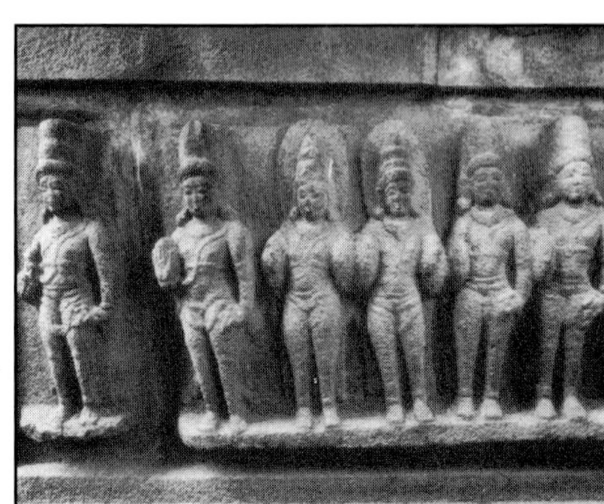

7 to 8 – Āditya s

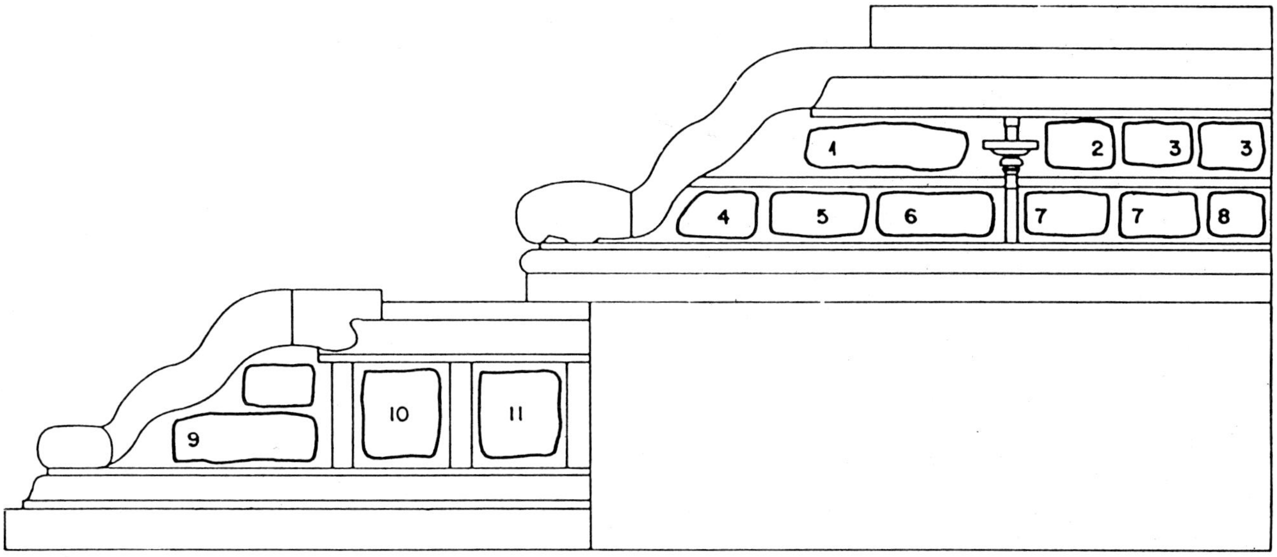

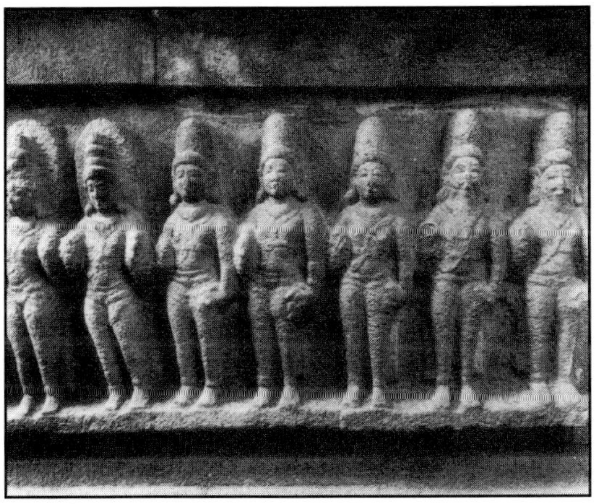

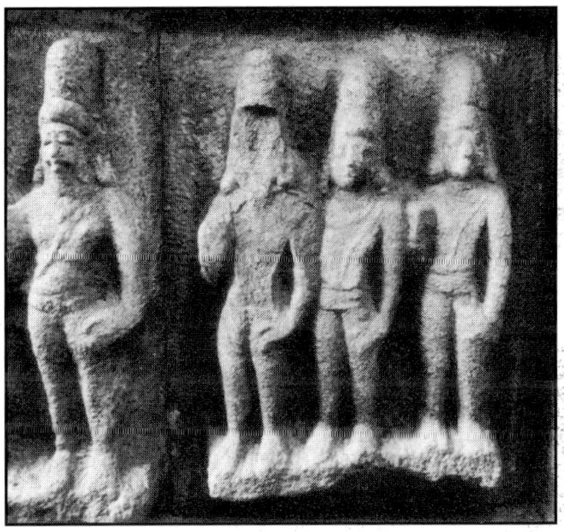

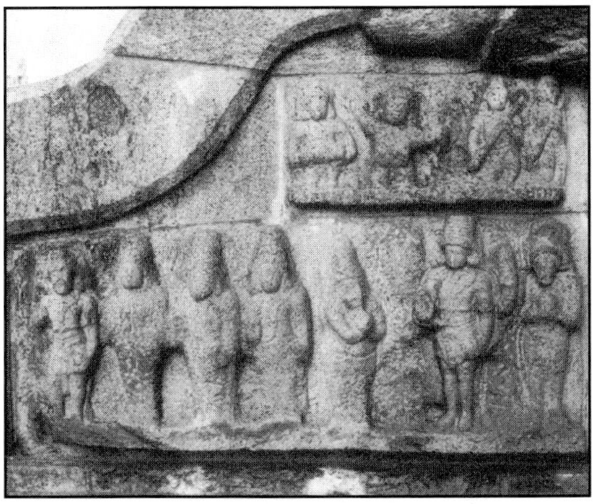

9 – Śiva and Dakṣa

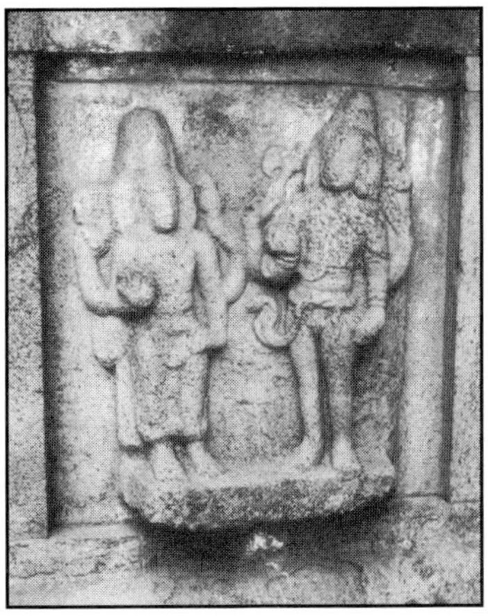

10 – Brahmā and Śiva

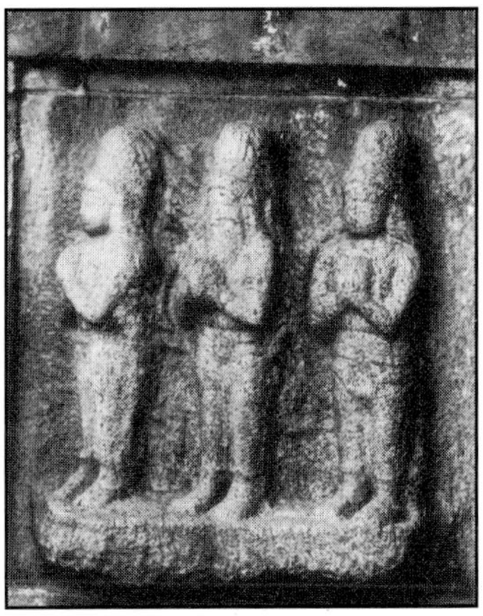

11 – Sages

Plate 12. Northern stairway of the vestibule, East face

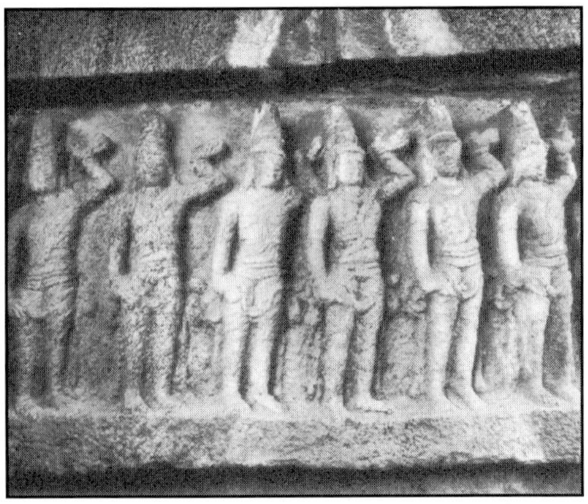

1 to 3 – Caṇḍeśānugrahamūrti

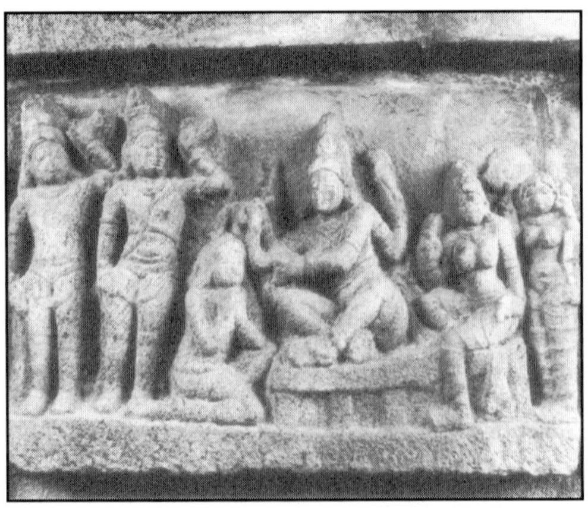

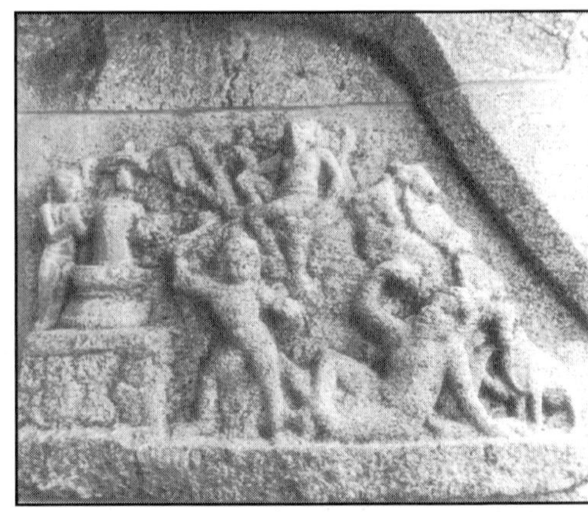

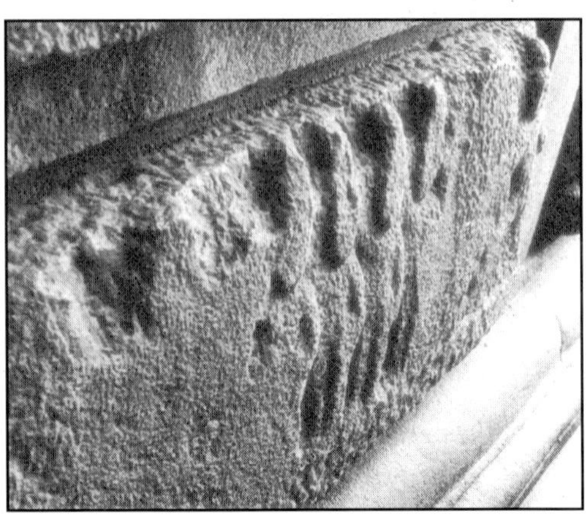

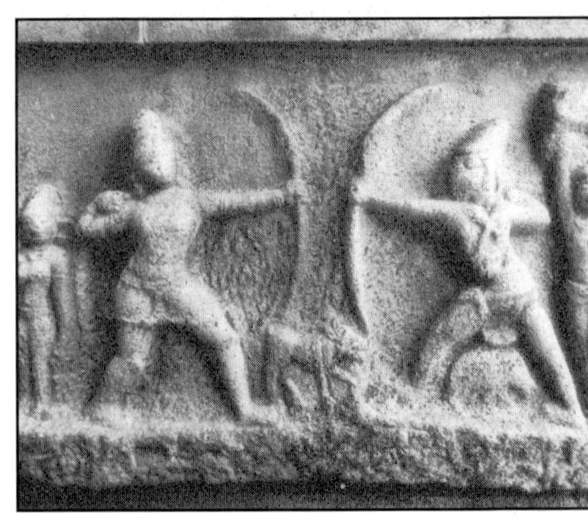

4 to 5 – Kirātārjunamūrti

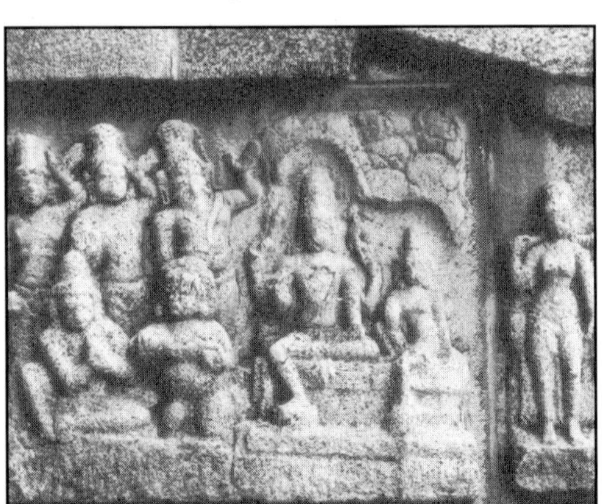

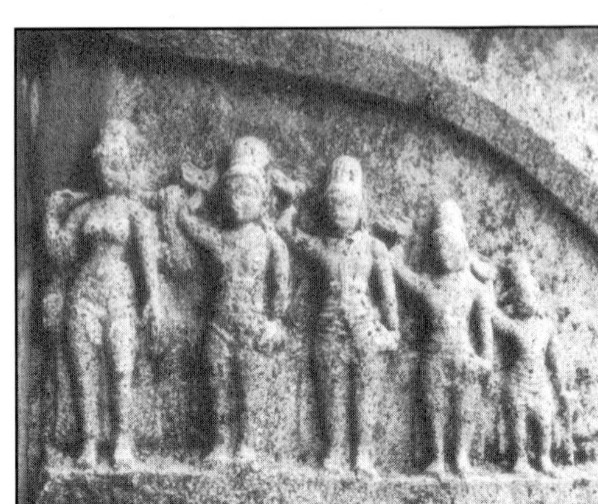

6 to 7 – Pāśupatāstradānamūrti

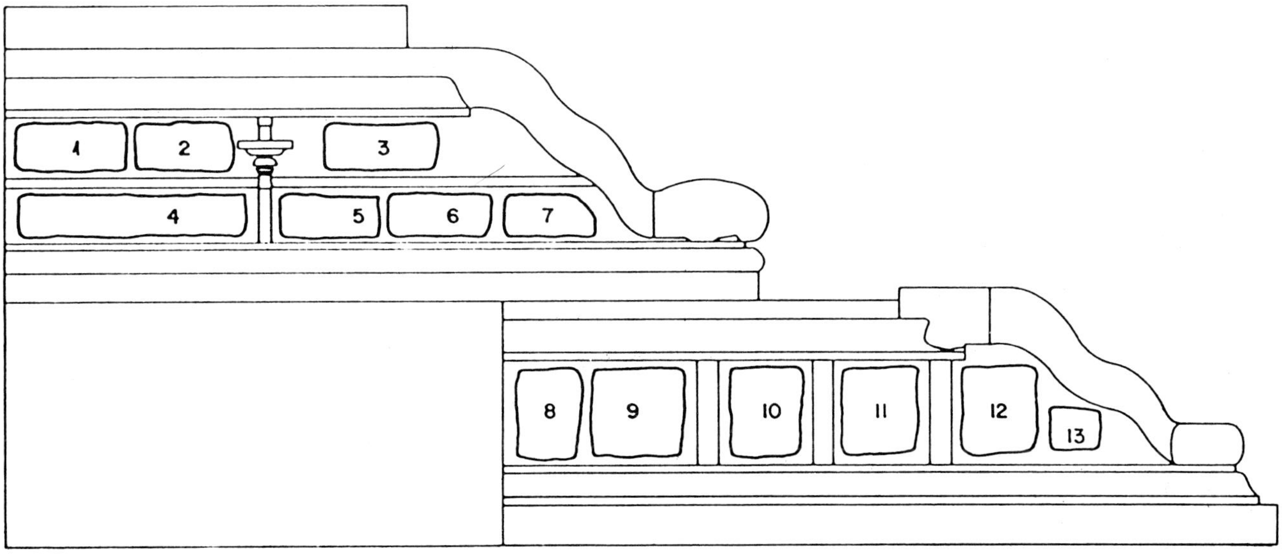

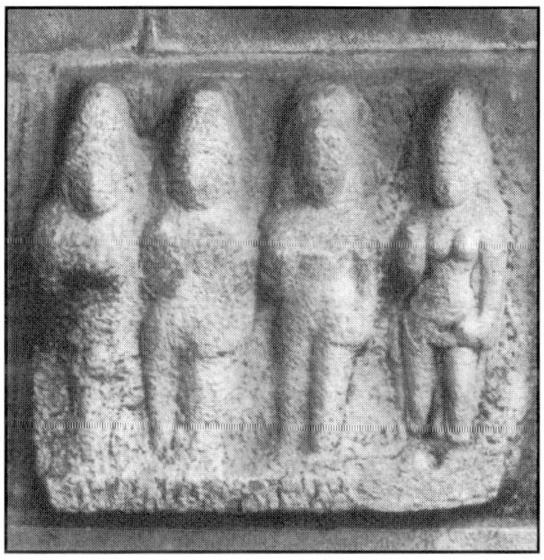

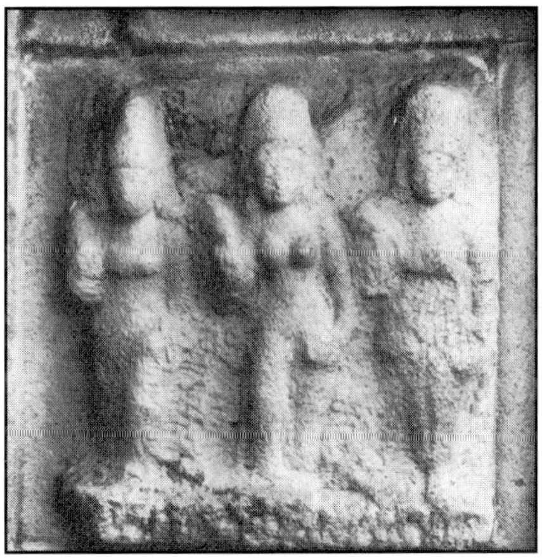

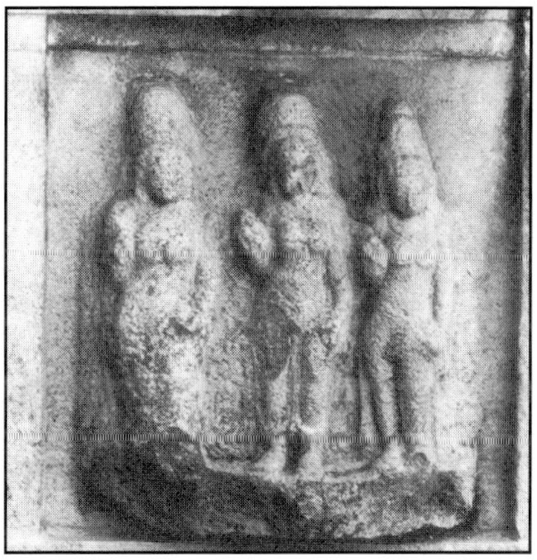

8 to 13 – Bhikṣāṭana and the ṛṣipatnīs

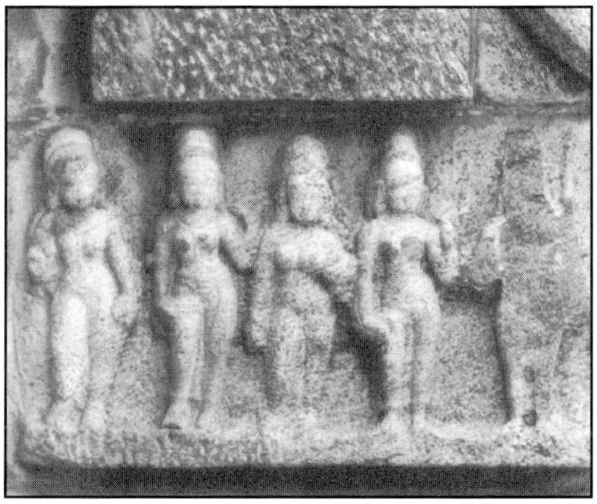

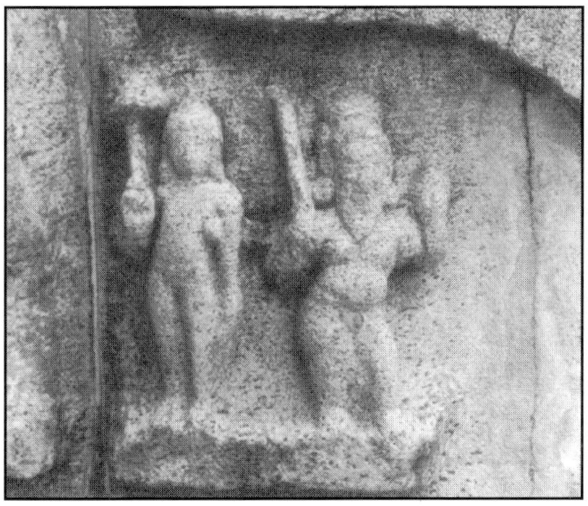

Plate 13. Inner gateway, eastern façade

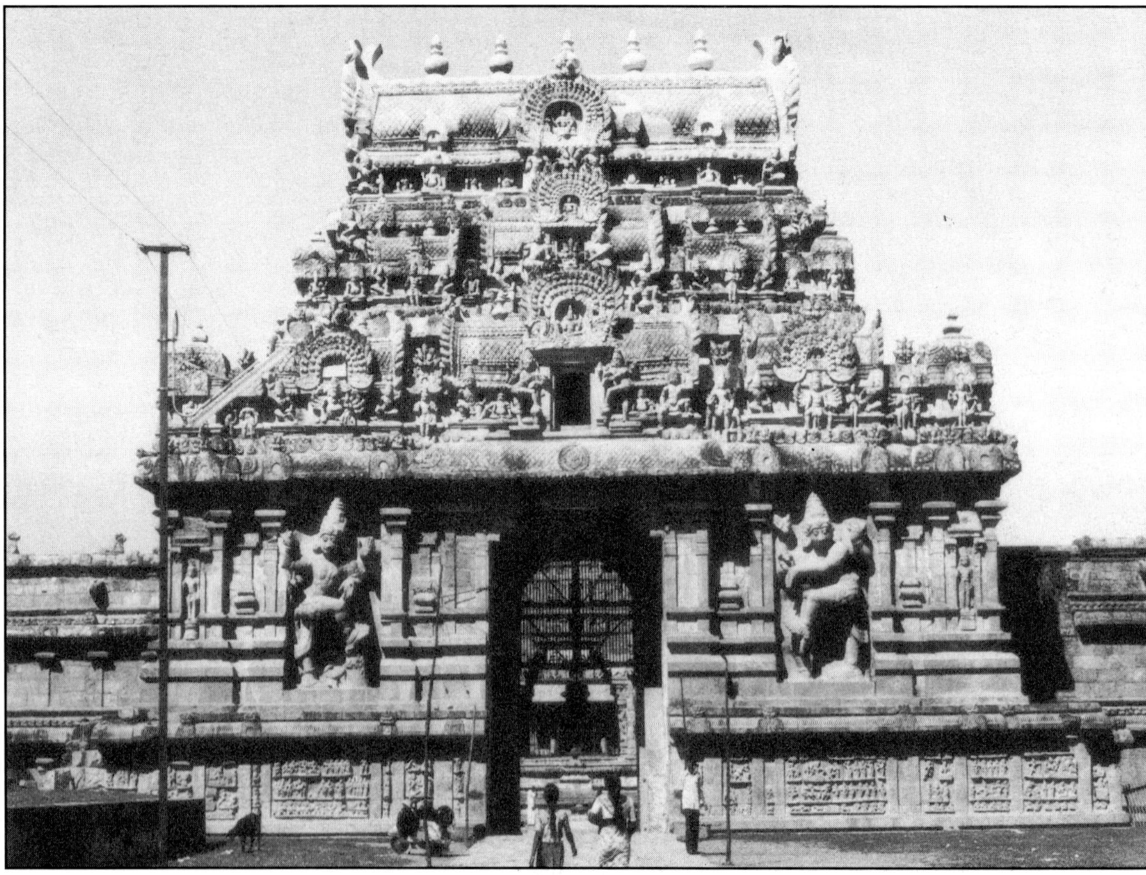

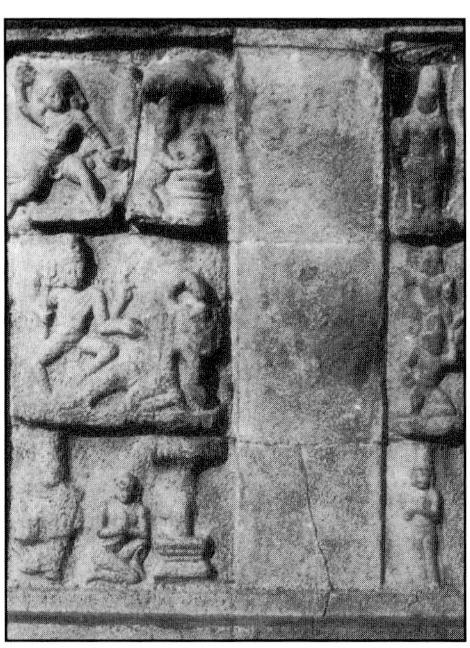

1 & 2 – Devotees, Kalāntaka

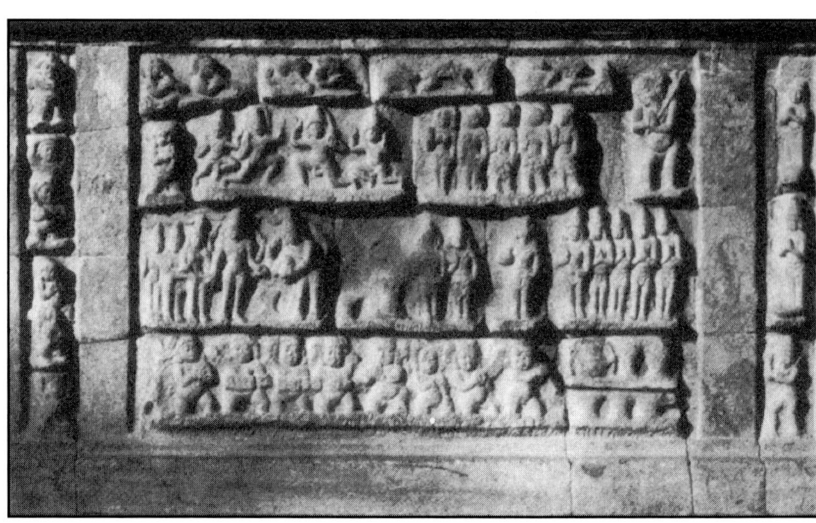

3 – Śiva's marriage

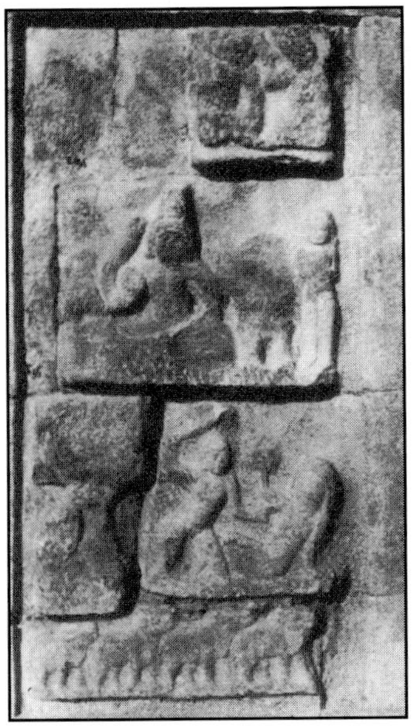

4. Caṇḍeśa

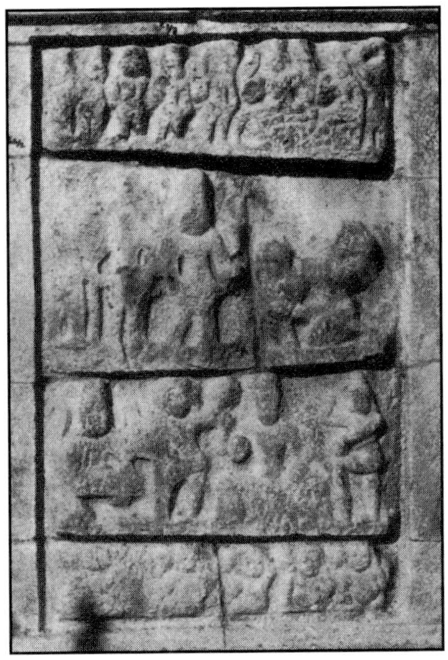

5. ?

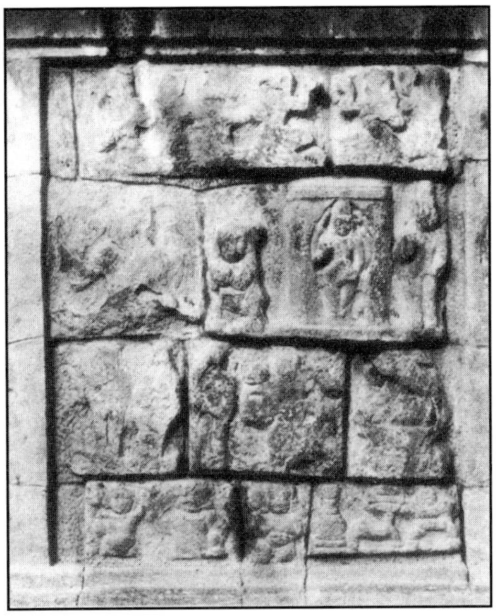

6. Liṅgodhbhava

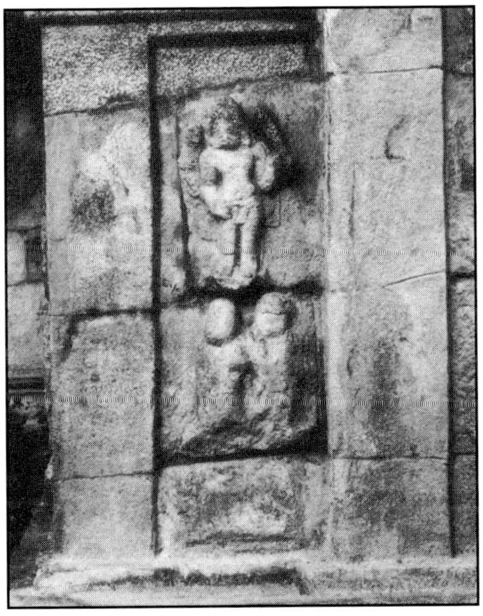

7. Caṇḍraśekhara

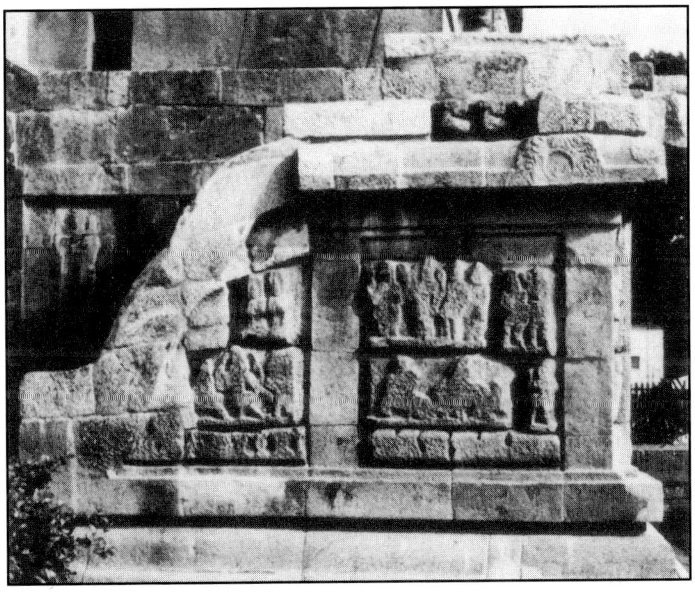

8 & 9. Sundarar and Cēramān Perumān

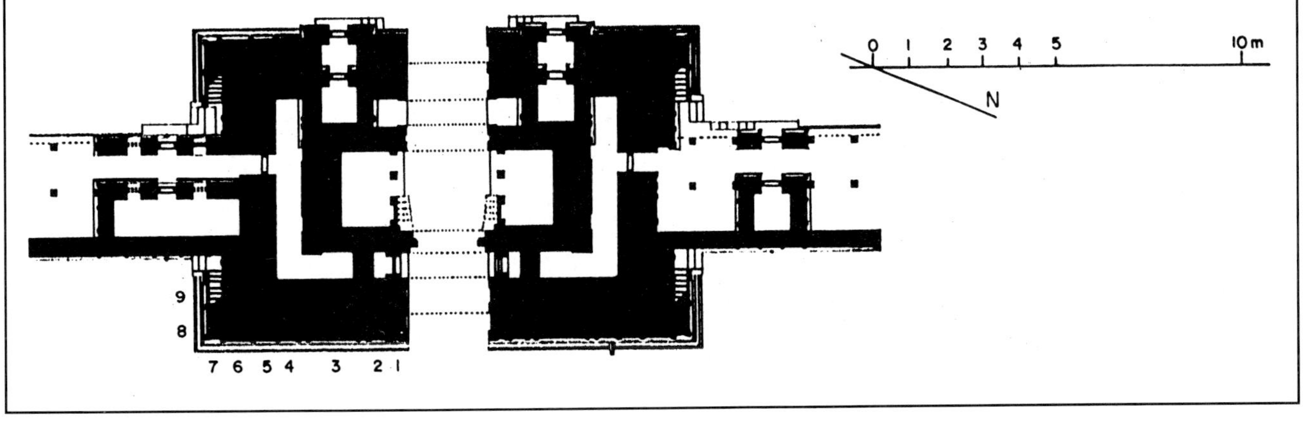

Plate 14. Inner gateway, eastern façade

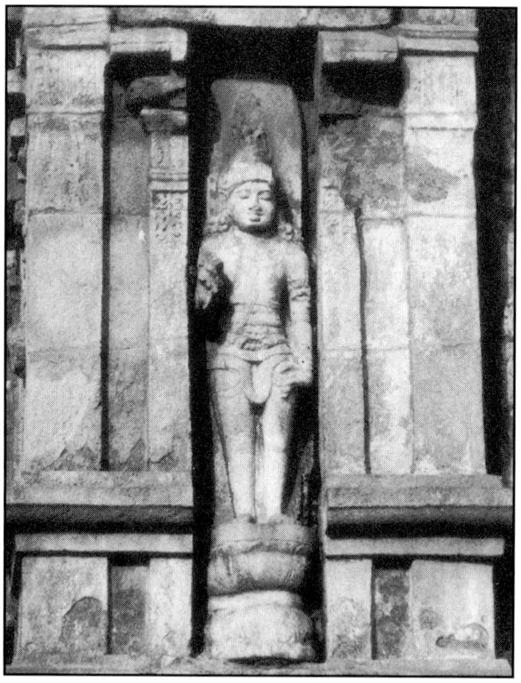

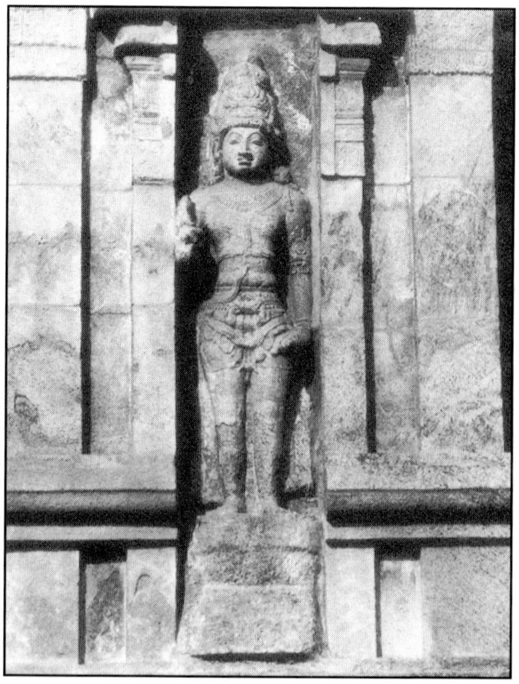

Sūrya and Chandra in niches of the main body

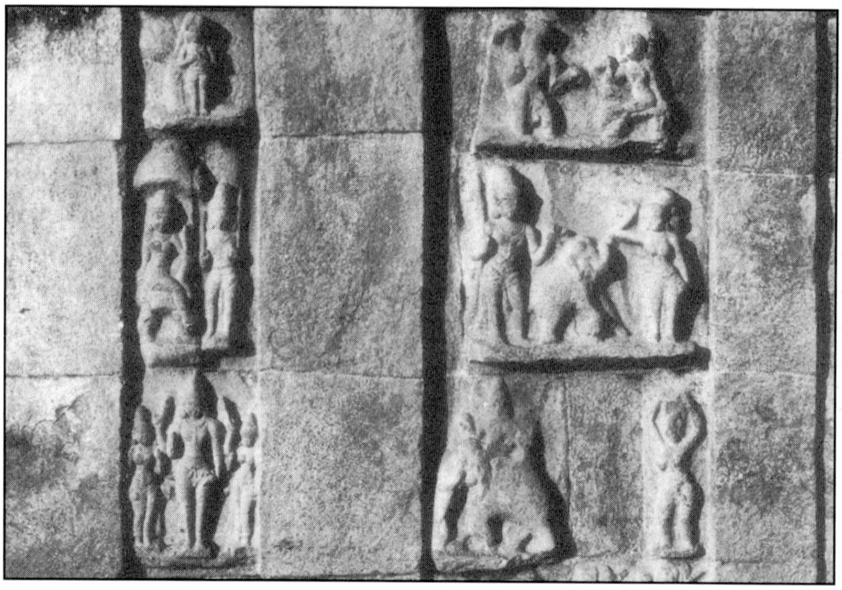

1 & 2. Subrahmaṇya and Vaḷḷi

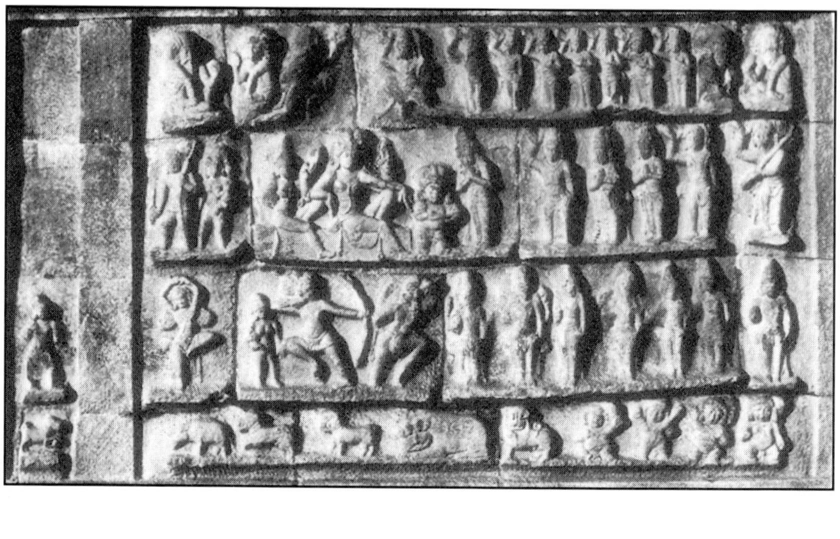

3. Pāśupatāstradānamūrti

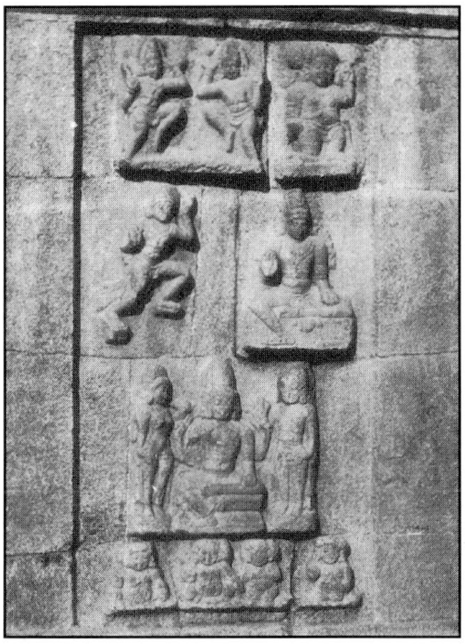

4. Brahmā

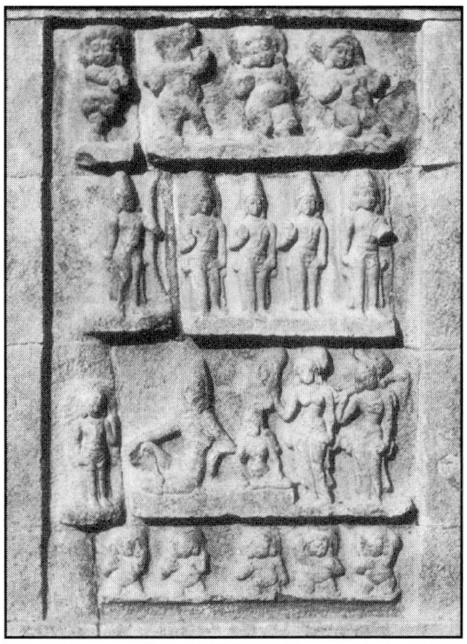

5. Pāṇḍavas and Indra

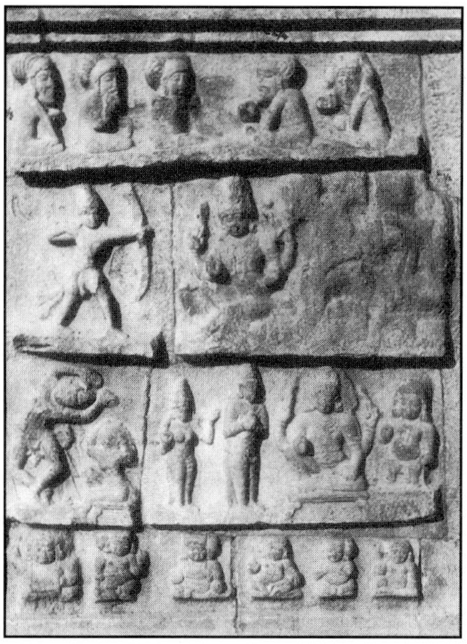

6. Kāmāntaka

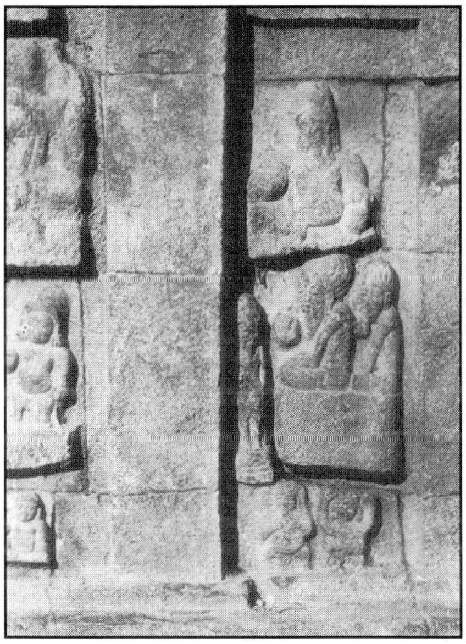

7. Sages

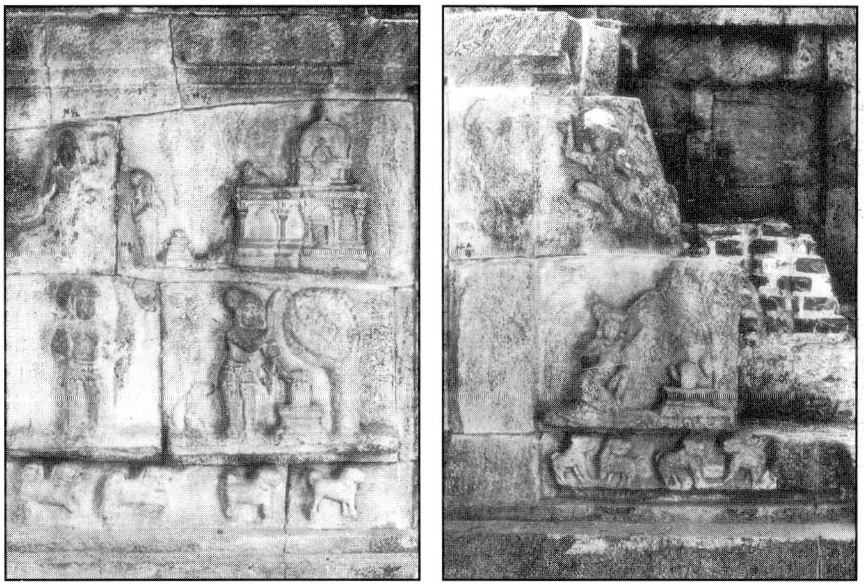

8 & 9. Kaṇṇappa Nāyanār

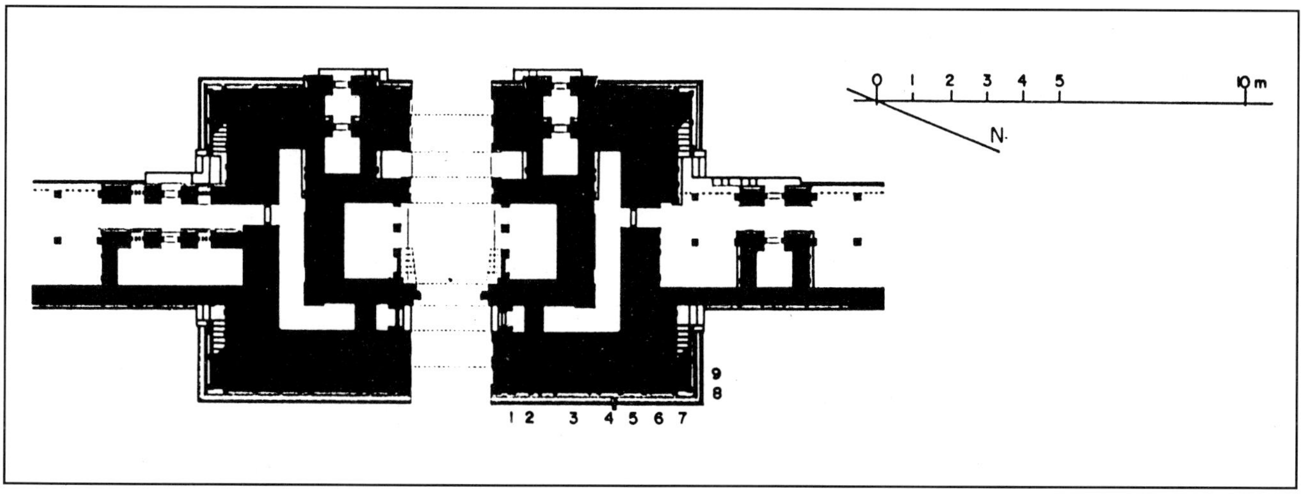

Plate 15. Inner gateway, western façade

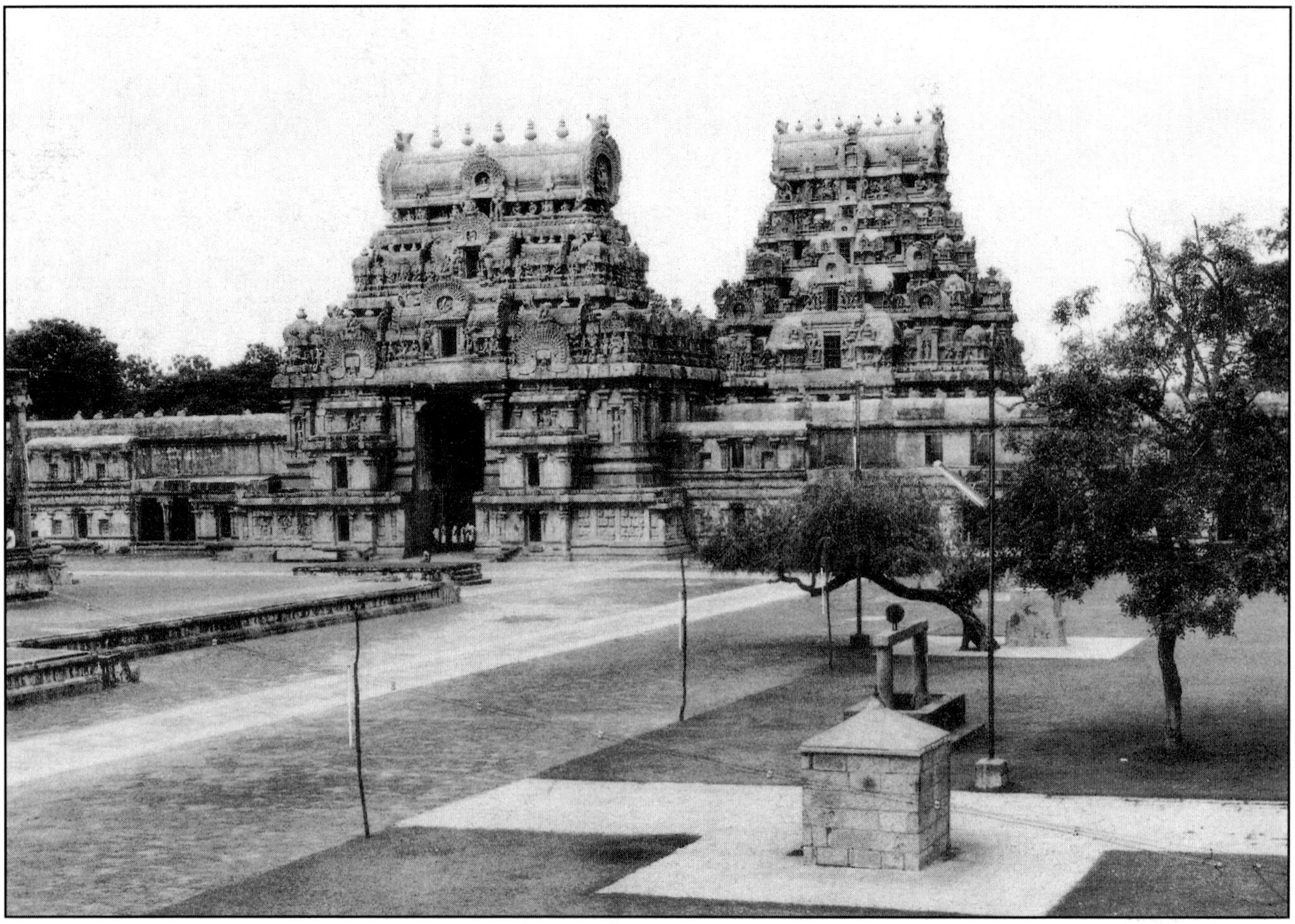

The two gateways from the courtyard

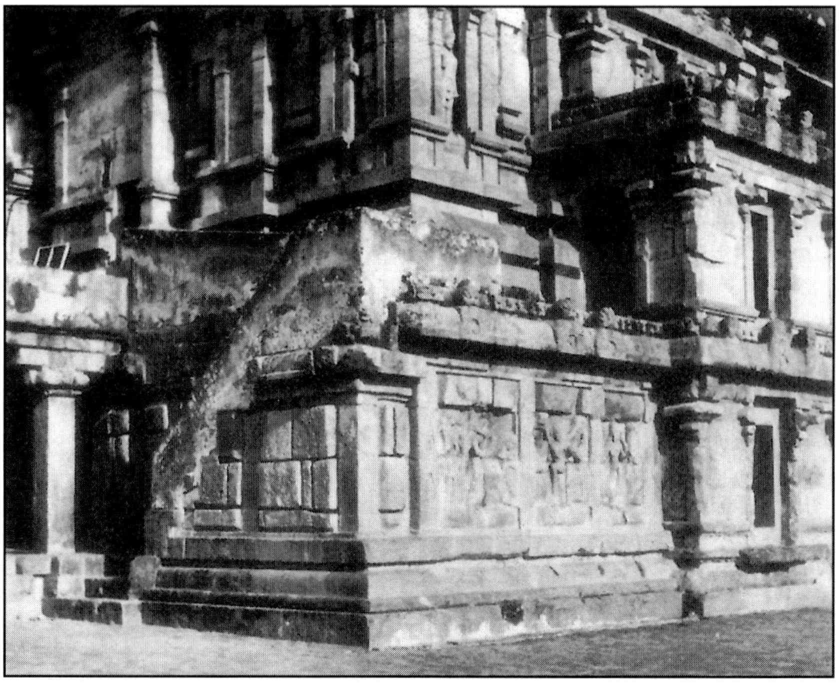

North-West corner

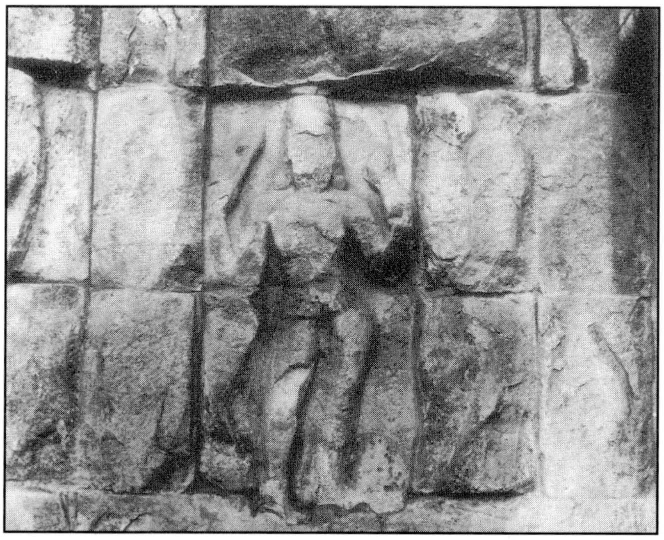

1. Chaṇḍraśekhara

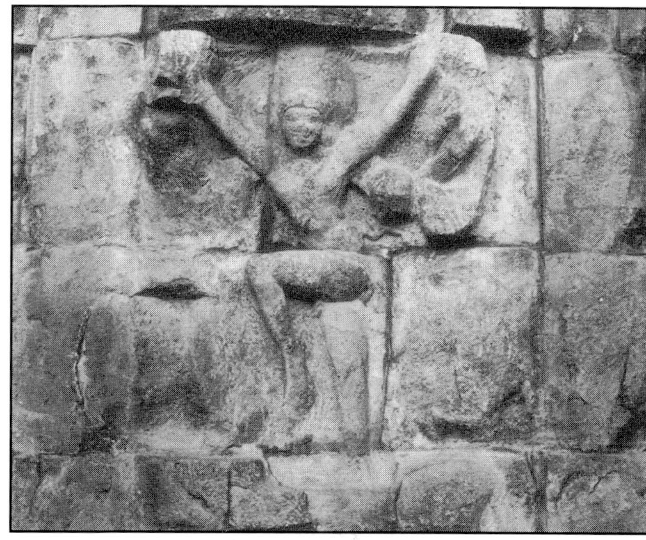

2. Gajāntaka

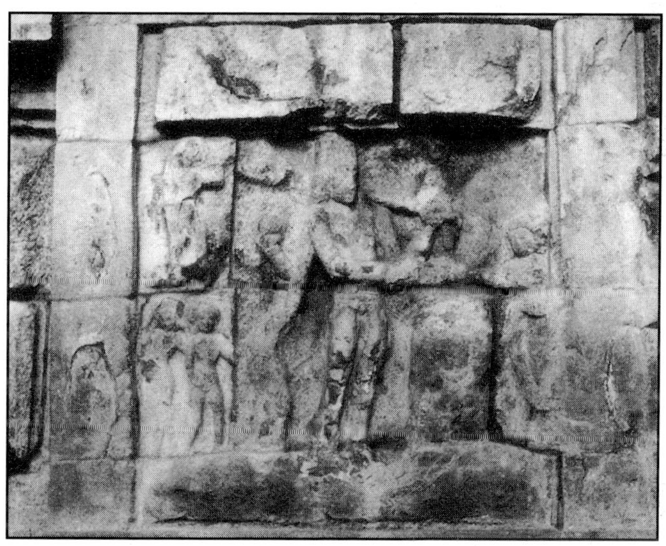

3. Bhikṣāṭana

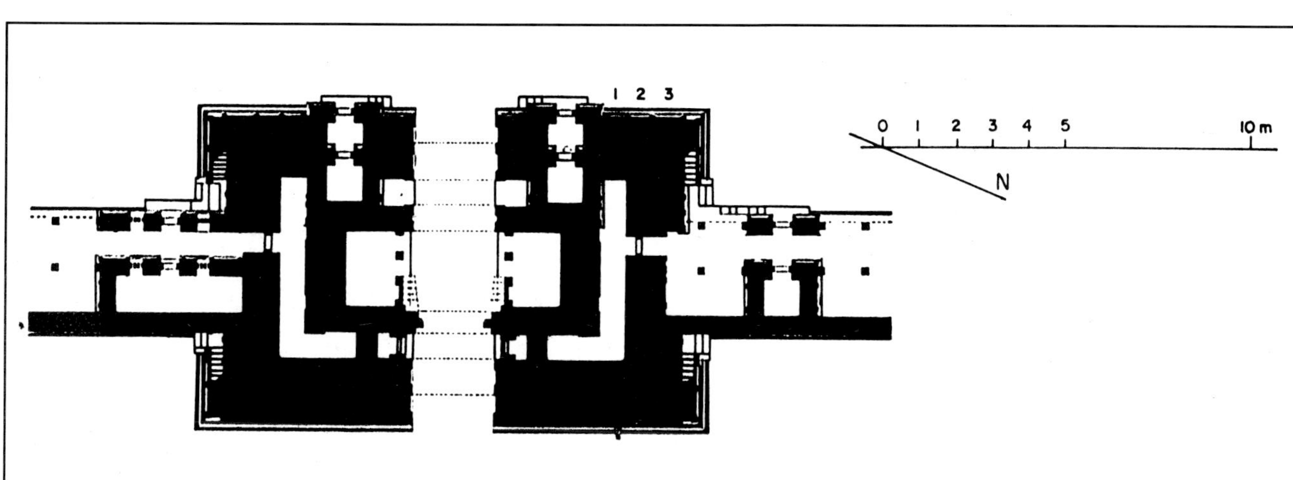

Plate 16. Inner gateway, western façade

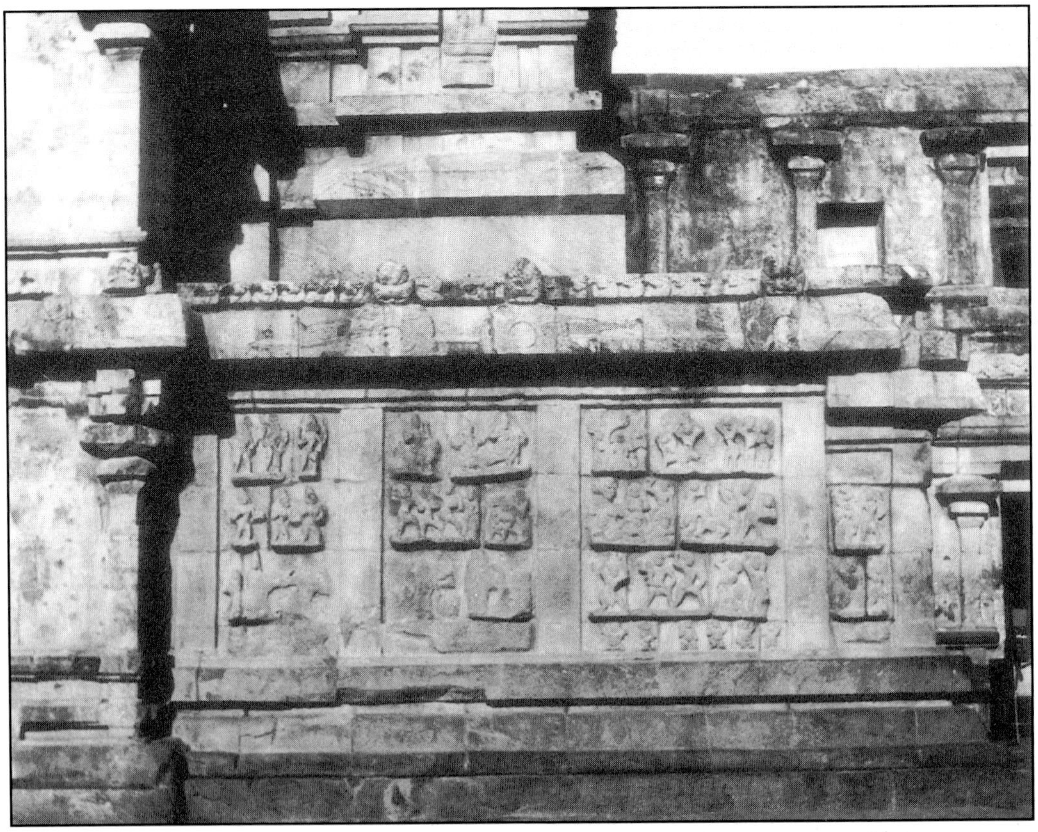

South-West corner of the gateway

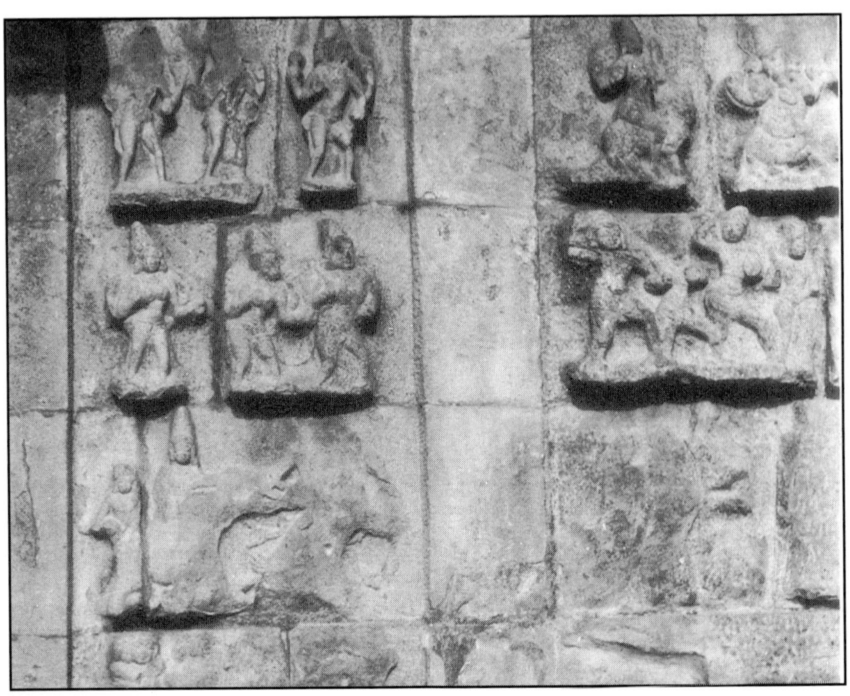

1 & 2. Gods on their mounts

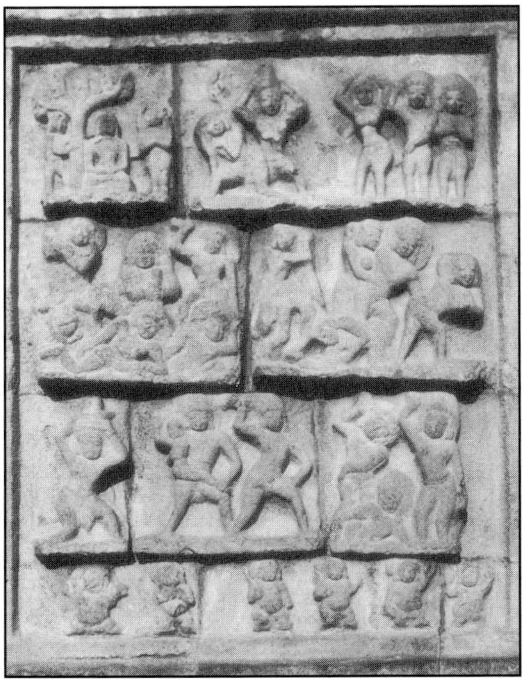

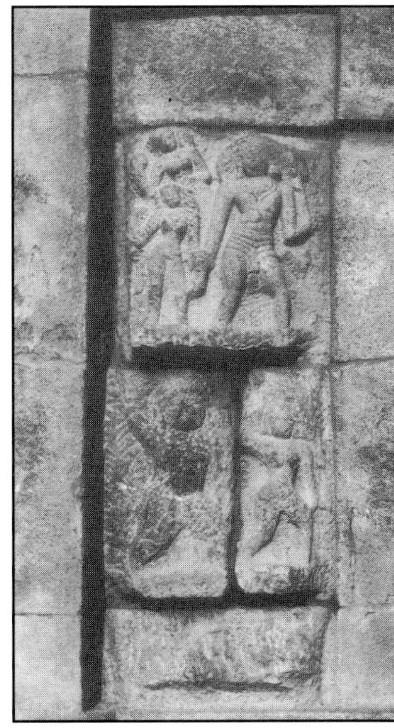

3 & 4. Buddha and the Tripuras

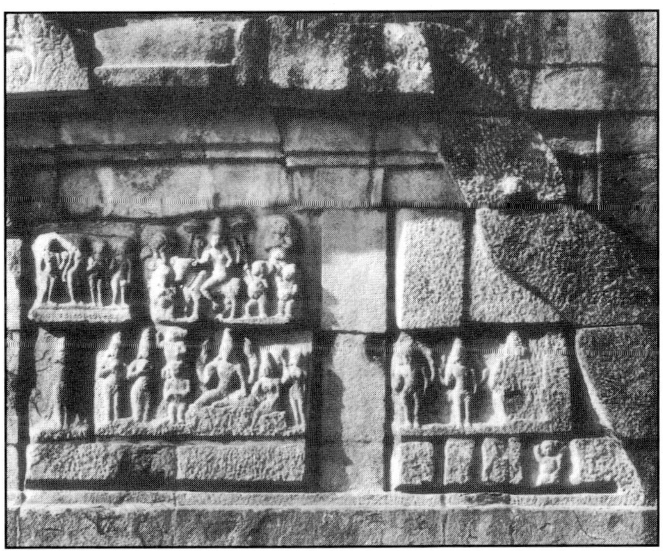

5 & 6. The Tripuras worshipping Śiva

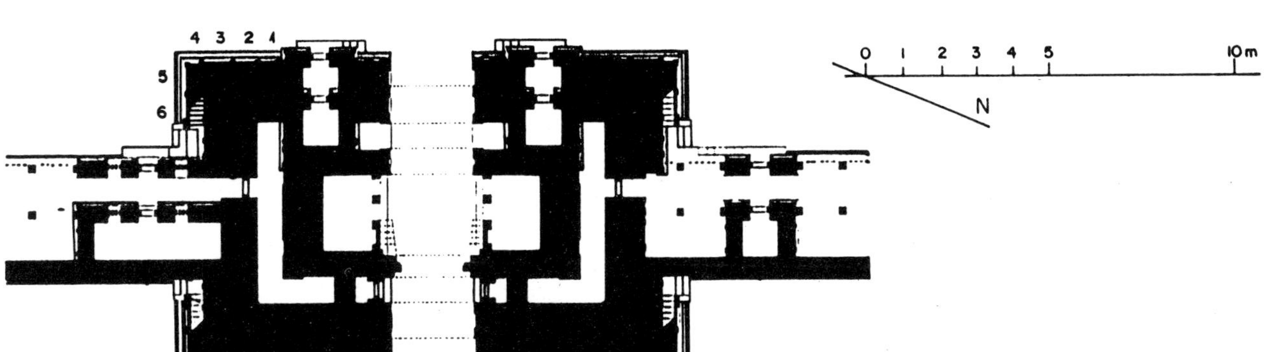

Plate 17. Subshrines of the gallery

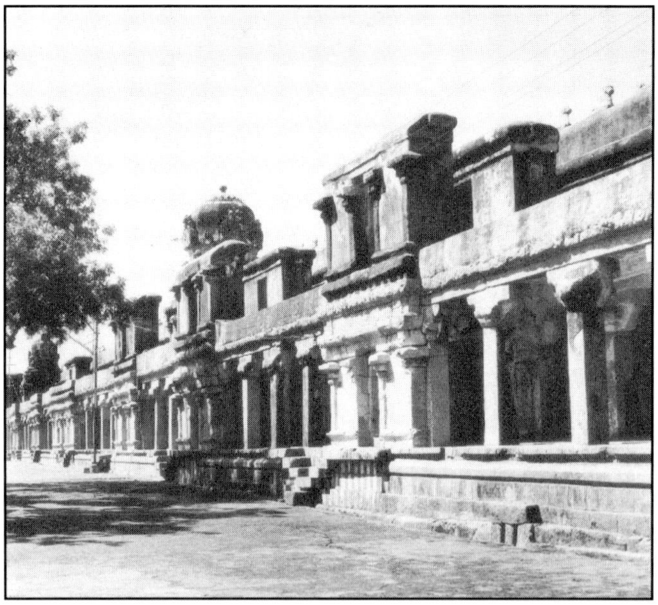

Subshrines of the gallery

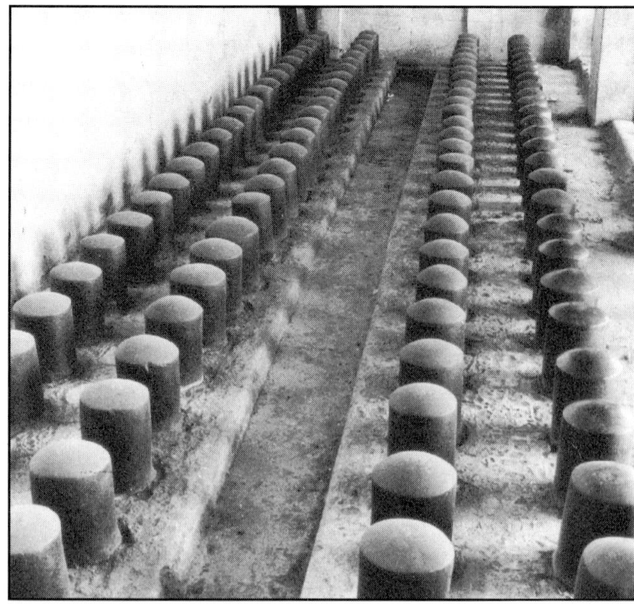

108 Liṅgas

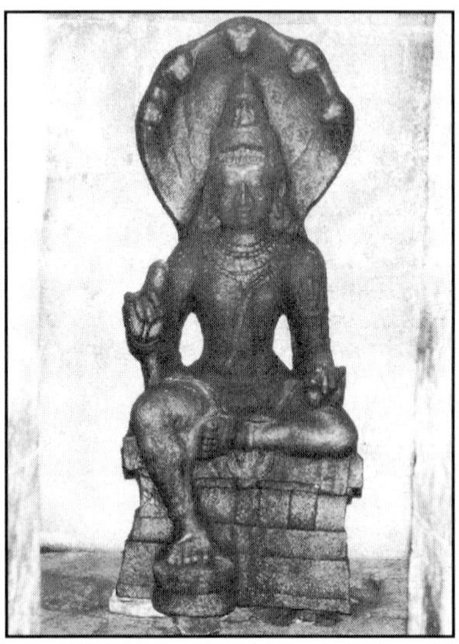

Nāgarāja

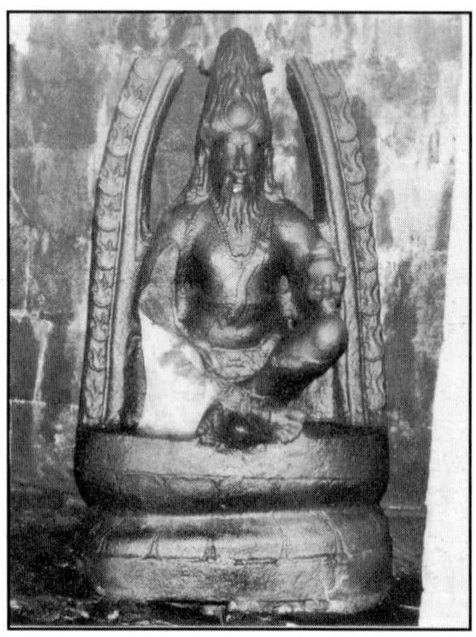

Agni

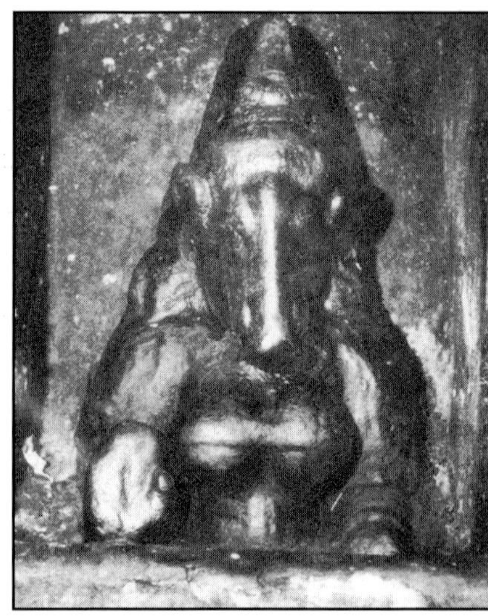

Varāhī

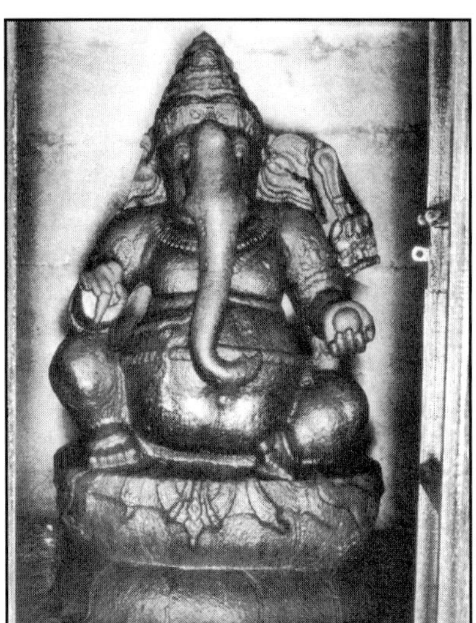

Gaṇapati

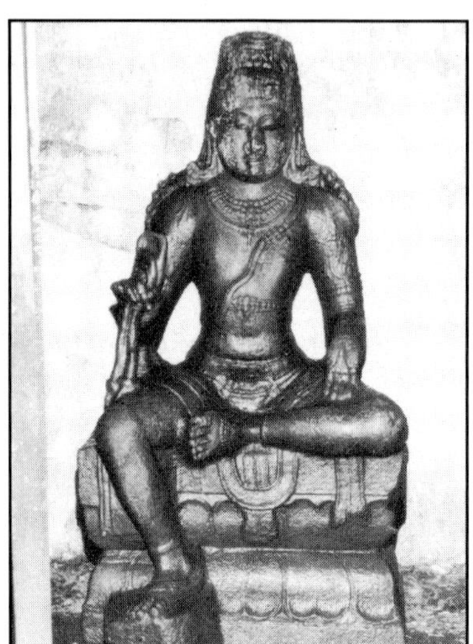

Varuṇa

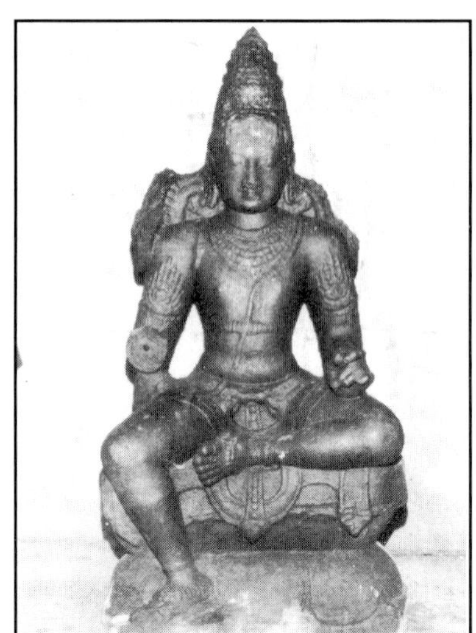

Vāyu

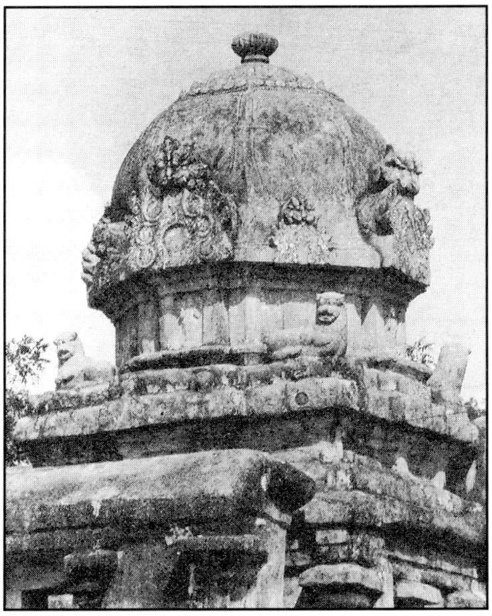

Soma

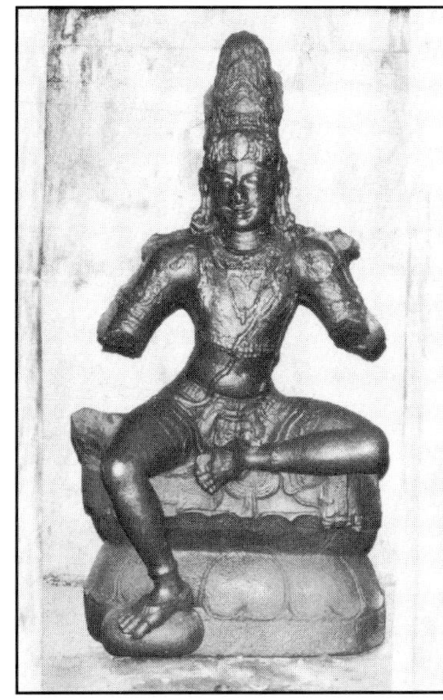

Īśāna

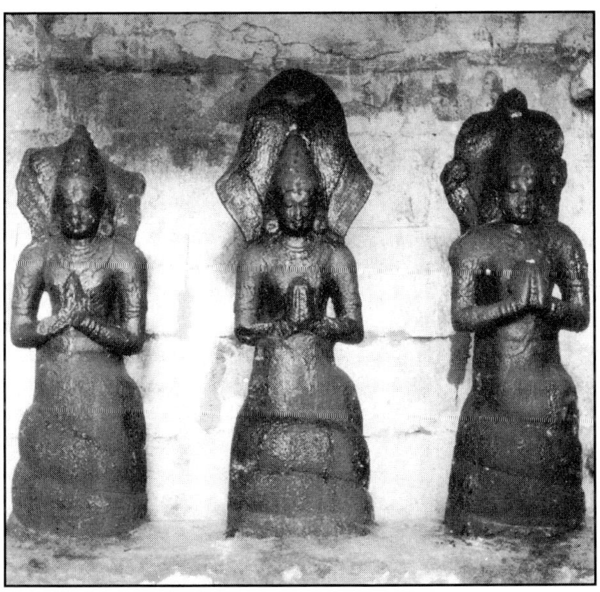

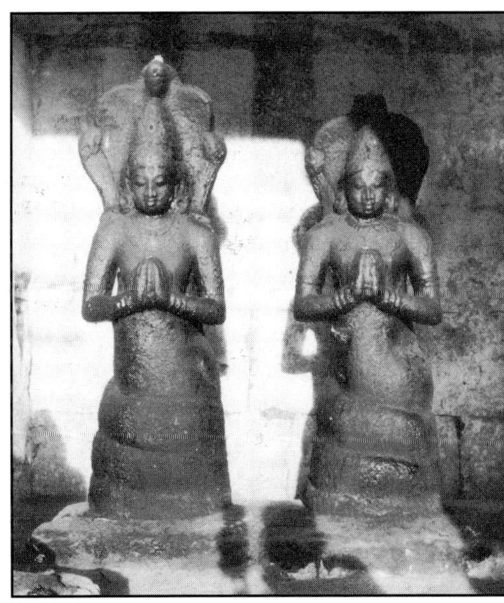

Nāgas

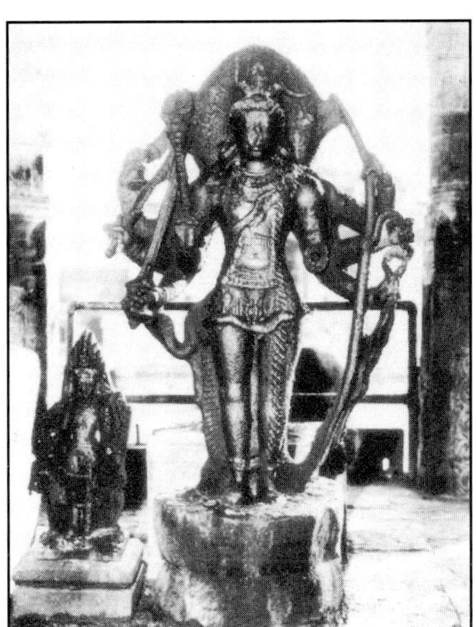

Bhairava

Plate 18. Architectural details

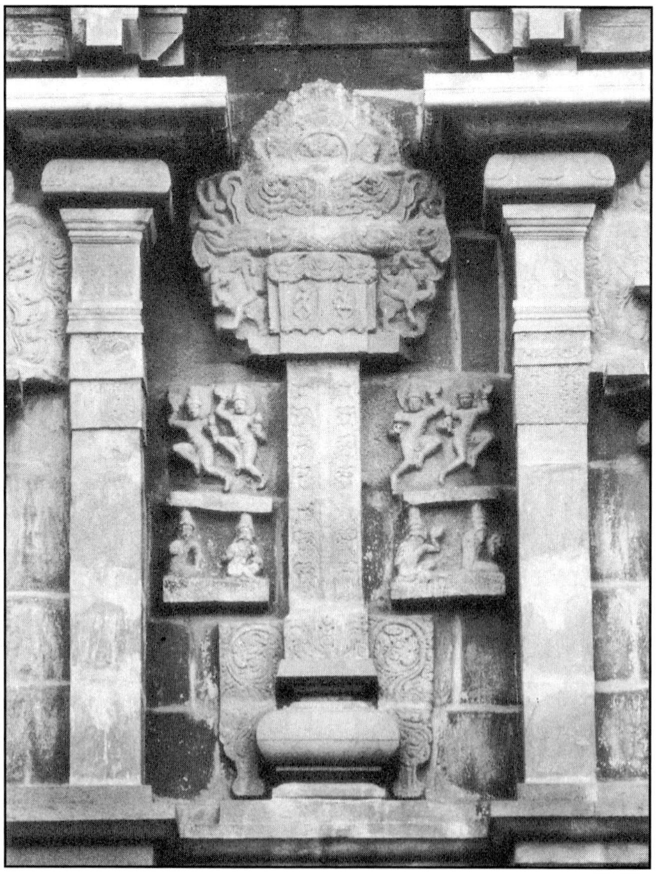

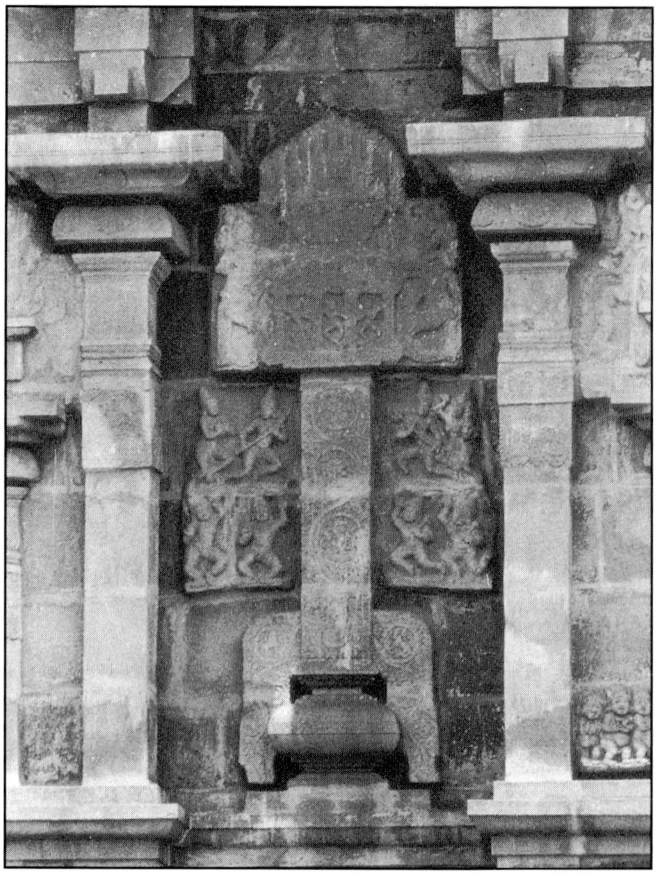

Sanctuary-tower: vase-pilasters, arcatures, blind dormer-windows

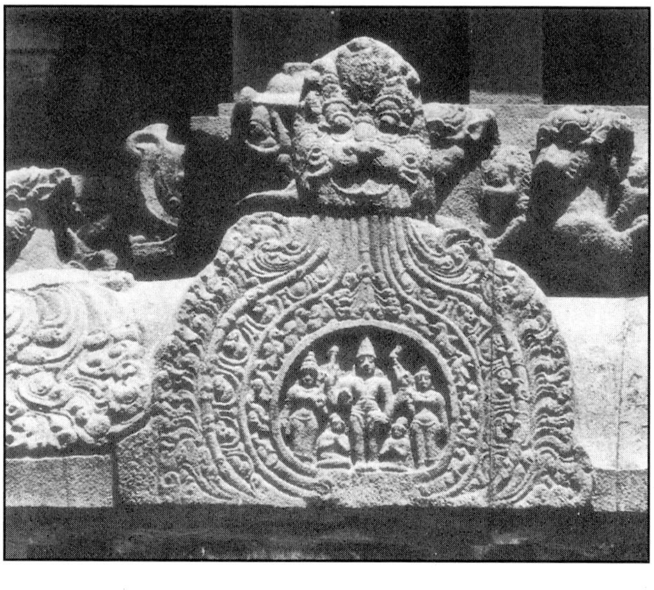

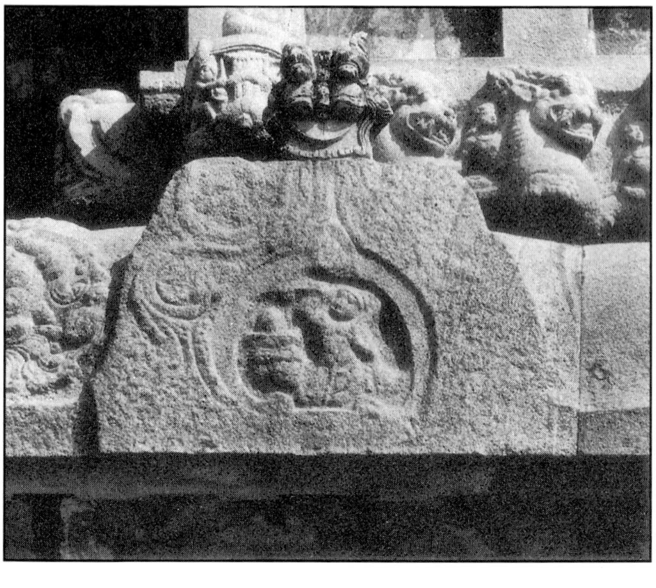

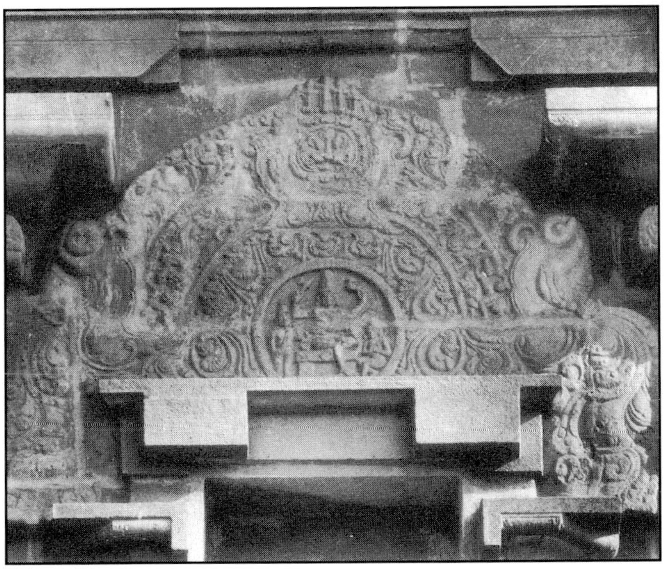

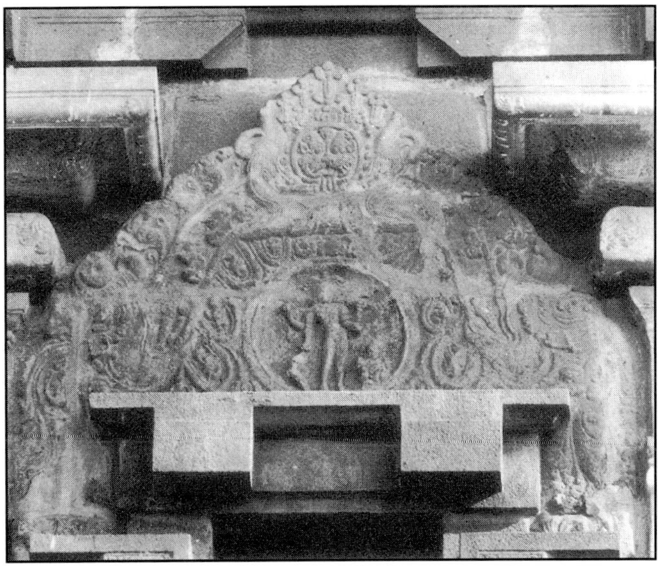

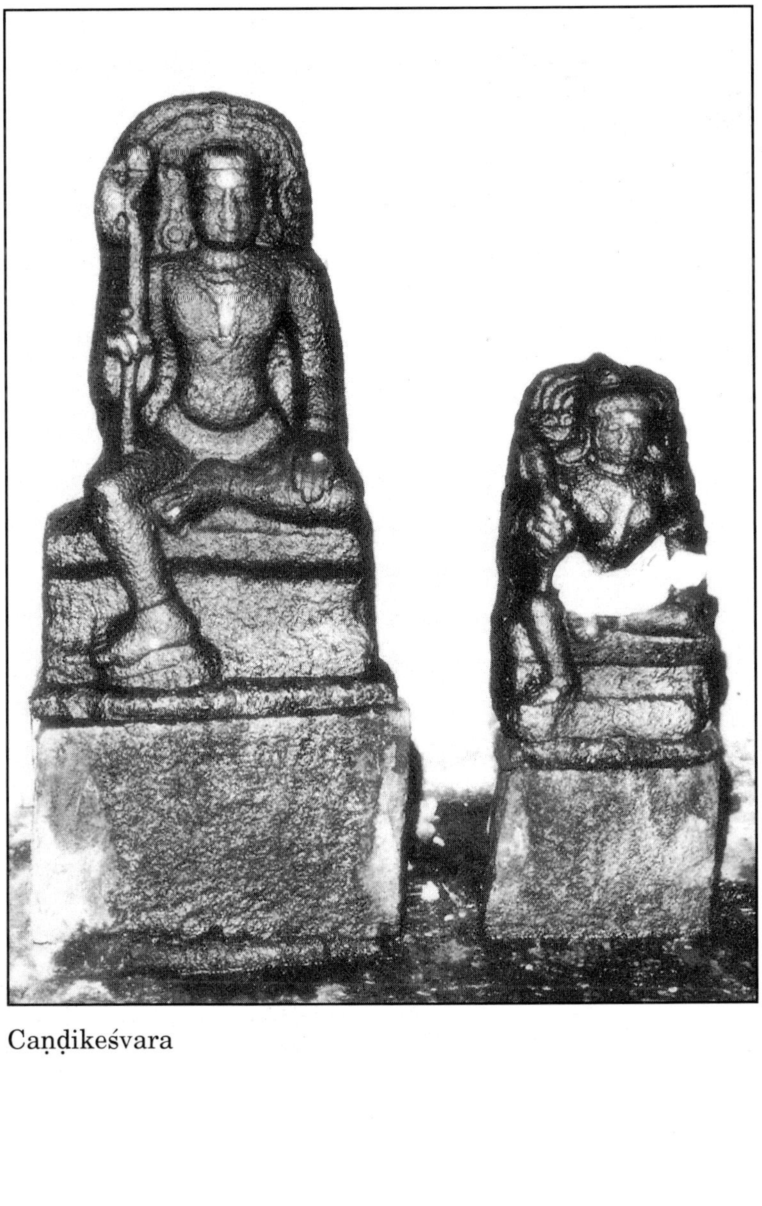

Caṇḍikeśvara

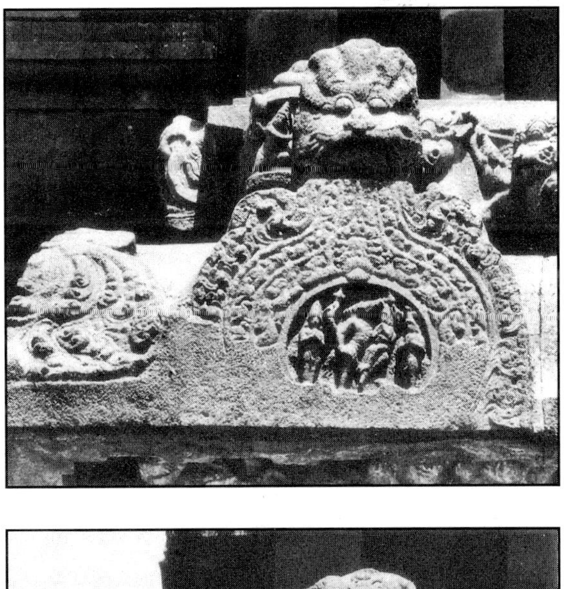

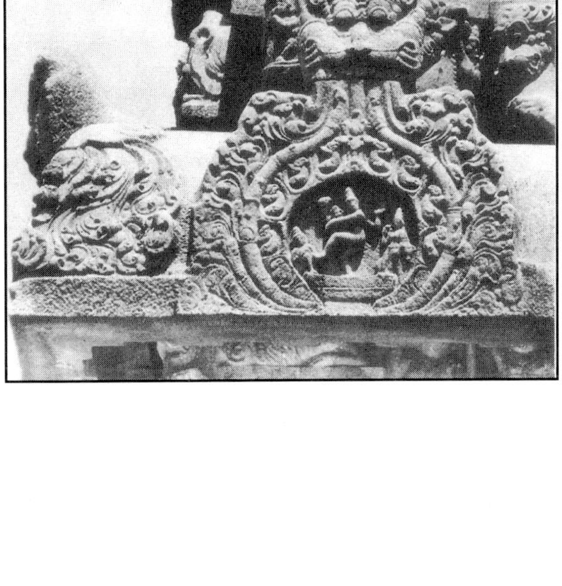